ANNUAL SHOWCASE

Creative Minds

Edited By Jenni Harrison

First published in Great Britain in 2022 by:

Young Writers
Remus House
Coltsfoot Drive
Peterborough
PE2 9BF
Telephone: 01733 890066
Website: www.youngwriters.co.uk

Printed and bound in the UK by BookPrintingUK
Website: www.bookprintinguk.com
YB0525F

Foreword

Since 1991, here at Young Writers we have celebrated the awesome power of creative writing, especially in children and young adults where it can serve as a vital method of expressing their emotions and views about the world around them.

Usually our creative writing competitions focus on either fiction or poetry in all its forms, but that does leave a gap for other writing skills and styles to fall through. What about all the writing that doesn't fit into either of those categories? Songs and scripts, blogs and book reviews, essays and articles; we wanted to read and celebrate those too! So we created the Annual Showcase, a competition where any style of writing could be submitted up to 1000 words.

Open to all 4-18 year-olds, the Annual Showcase was the perfect opportunity for any budding young writer, or their proud parent or teacher, to submit a piece of writing on any topic and in any style. The extended word limit also allowed these authors to write at length, really exploring their ideas and imagination.

All the entries we've received have been a delight to read. On every topic conceivable, in every style, they prove that these young writers are bursting with ideas and creativity; we just need to give them an outlet! We really hope we've done that with the Annual Showcase, and we hope that you enjoy reading them as much as we have!

Contents

THE CREATIVE WRITING

Billy

B right
I ntellectual
L oving when looking after younger students in school
L oyal to my friends
Y oung.

B E

Ash Meadow School, Sutton Manor

Dylan

D etermined
Y oung
L oving
A dventurous
N ice.

Dylan Lowry (13)
Ash Meadow School, Sutton Manor

Ewan

E nergetic

W onderful

A mazing

N ice.

E P (11)

Ash Meadow School, Sutton Manor

The Silence

The white-haired child was only too glad to make it back home. After all that grief and sorrow she suffered lashing out on the window as rain; the inside feeling just as mild as the outside was savage. The girl didn't know it at the time, but this would be the last time she would see the outside in a very long time.

Shortly after the girl had devoured every sherbet in the bowl, her ruby-pink eyes were set on her mother, fast asleep on the sofa. The warmth of home fogged around the lounge, wandered into the kitchen, upstairs, downstairs... Lingered above the child's eyelids, whispering into her ear; encouraging her to sleep. To rest and fall into a world that let her float, let her fly away into an endless dream. And the girl was going to.

But suddenly, her mother burst like a balloon, quite literally too. It seemed that the dreams had come to the girl instead. The walls around her melted, ceilings bounced and lights popped, the very fabric of reality tearing apart. Curtains engulfed the windows, walls shrouded the curtains, checked black and white squares fractured the floor; floral creatures and eyes clambered up to form a new ceiling. The girl wondered whether she was already in a dream, asleep, but her breathing, consciously told her this was no illusion.

"What in the wide world is going on?" she uttered to herself. "Mummy? Are you okay?"

She made to dart up to her, but the minute she spun around she was met, face to face, with a peculiar... human? No... this was no human. It was a creature, or a monster, with a body so elongated it looked like it had been stretched to almost reach the ceiling.

4

It was shrouded in an inky-black coat of fur; cloaked in a greying waistcoat that appeared rather ruffled indeed. All was grey up to its multicoloured ruff, erupting with ruby reds and ripping oranges and opulent purples.

Plastered onto its face, was not a face at all; but a ghostly white mask with the most abnormally, overgrown nose and two black knobs of eyes that stared off in different directions. Although such a look was intended to amuse the observer, to the girl, it did not. On the contrary, it emitted an uneasiness inside the child. And so this faceless, furry thing bent so low its entire nose encaptured the girl's entire circle of vision.

A scrawny hand with a white glove curled around her, holding a sign bearing the word: *Treatment?* And at this, the girl screamed.

No. Not after the incident in the hospital this night; the fire, the vile wretches of the doctors; the human experimentation, the suffering; could persuade the girl that this monster wasn't going to do something foul too? Its open hand, its benign posture did not outweigh the overwhelming instinct, tugging at the girls' guts, that this creature was not a friend.

At her heels, the girl took off to the door nearest to her; opening it and, to her surprise, fell off the cliff of the last fragment of reality into a rabbit hole she will not climb out of. This was supposed to be the dining room. It was supposed to have a docile three-dimensional room intact with ceilings and floors. Then why was the girl, instead, flying through the mangling fractions of space and time; plummeting, never touching, spiralling into a hurricane of chaos?

Eyes swelling out of threaded frames, ants conquering over giants in the undepictable horizon. Imprints of screams and giggles etched out of the indefinite floor she couldn't see. Senses and smells coiled around the girl's nostrils, flaring them with the breath of fire...

The child looked up to check the clock; yet the clock was on the cooking pan being fried by a balloon-headed imp. Black was white. It wasn't until the girl hit rock bottom of this no longer room that the never-ending screams of madness softened slightly. She was in a deafening silent room cloaked in black. The poor girl was knocked off her feet in the midst of such surprising colours and cackles; that she had quite forgotten she even had them. She picked herself up.

"Daisy..." It was a crawling, raking shell of a voice that brought the girl to remember that her name was, in fact, Daisy.

Her head spun around for the owner of this dark and dreary hum in a room that seemed before so lifeless. Her eyes rolled upon it. A steel-tight cage was suspended by the ceiling, border with thick bars and inside it; seemed to be a black bird? But it couldn't be, for it had goat hooves. Yet it was no goat; for it stood, and shaped and spoke like a human.

It was enveloped in a ragged, grey robe; its arms crossed concealing its hands. The chalky, naked beak was the only part that separated it from the encircling darkness around it; as white as Daisy's hair. Its beaky pretence reminded the girl of something she read from the history books once; yet she could not seem to pin it into conscience.

"Who on earth are you, mister bird?" uttered Daisy all of the courage she could muster. "And... Why are you in my home? In that cage?"

She could distinguish two minuscule dots of the monster's eye glittering out at her as it listened to her wispy voice.

"This is not your home anymore, Daisy. It has been infected by a plague, an illness in your head."

"Sorry to say, mister, but... how do you know my name?" The poor girl's voice was thinning for every second spent with this creature. The air around her too seemed to vanish into the dark.

"Because I have heard," the creature continued, "The Hungry Thing's ideas. It's looking for a new child, it's looking for you."

The child didn't understand what any of this meant, she fiddled with one of her pigtails feebly. "What... What hungry thing?"

"The Hungry Thing, the creator of this world. It's long and furry and wears a ruff, with a white mask and a big long nose. It's come to get you, Daisy. You need to leave before it does. It will try to 'cure' you. You need to leave before you catch the plague, and end what should have never happened a long time ago."

Whenever Daisy's voice weakened, the monster's voices thickened with dreariness. The lonesome child failed to recognise whether the shivers crawling up her spine were from cold, or something else. The sudden lack of presence of her mum now began to wash over her; tears crept out of her rosy-red eyes as her cheeks froze. She just wanted to go home. The silence of no family fogged over her mind like a grey cloud as her figure lay still.

7

And it was the creature who spoke again: "If you let me out of this cage, I will help you."

Miriam Sanyal (16)
Beech Hall School, Tytherington

Behind The Fence Of Thorns

I can see things nobody else can, and they shun me for it. Ridicule me. Ostracise me.

If only they could open their eyes for even a second to see the wonderful monstrosities that I see. They would be breathless and mortified to see the smouldering holes in the sky, to see the world in colour. Yes, that's something only I see. Colour is a figment of the delusional child's imagination, as the adults say.

The days here are monotonous, like a never-ending loop, and I would give anything to leave this place. Anything. The grey school days move at the pace of a drunken snail, the teacher's toneless voice reverberating against the bleak walls. The other children just glide through it. If only I could give them a taste of how colourful life could be. But they refuse to acknowledge anything other than... this.

I amble down the stairs, ready to leave for school. My mother is asleep on the sofa. She seems to be doing that a lot lately; guess we're back to keeping secrets.

My father moved to the city last year with my sister, and we've lost contact since then. I do know my sister's published two fantasy novels since, both set in a place called England. Both are on my shelf, in pristine condition. They're all I have left of her.

When I get to the school gates, I realise how early it is. I'm the first one here, and the sun has barely appeared over the horizon yet.

Time for a detour.

I slowly step backwards from the school gate, then break into a sprint. I know exactly where I'm going. The wooden fence materialised at the edge of the village about a week ago, and I've been desperate for a chance to investigate it since. After all, I'm the only one who can see it. The fence is about six feet tall and made of splintered wood that resembles thorns. I walk along the length of the fence, and eventually, I find a concealed gate. I gently push it open and stick my head through the gap. The shadows of the tallest buildings I've ever seen fall onto me. Towers climbing towards the sky, like a rotten hand clawing its way out of a grave. Palaces larger than the village, structures I feel embarrassed to be around. Mansions that have been cut out of a history book.

The things I've always dreamed about. I wander, dumbfounded, between the breathtaking structures. But it's not only buildings. The sky is whole. There are trees taller than the towers, rushing rivers clearer than the glimmering glass windows of the castles, and blankets of grass. The most beautiful grass I've ever seen. Vibrant and soft-looking, speckled with wildflowers.

Grass like this doesn't exist beyond that fence; nor do these buildings or colours. This is an entirely different world, separated from the crying, grey wasteland by a fence of wooden thorns. I know one thing for certain: I'm never going back. Something about this place seems so enticing. It's lured me into its grip, and I couldn't be more grateful.

I gasp. What about Mother? I should go back to see her, one last time. I won't miss her, but it would be rude to just disappear. Frantically, I scramble back towards the village. I burst through the door of my mother's derelict cottage.

"Mother?"

The only reply I get is thundering silence. I suppose she's gone out. I leap up the stairs and collect my sister's novels from my shelf, go back downstairs, grab an apple from the kitchen, and leave. I decide to go to the village square - my mother's most likely there. I reach the brow of the hill that overlooks the village square. I drop my apple.

No.

My apple rolls down the hill, building up speed until it crashes into a pile of stiff, pale limbs. Faces frozen in fear, empty eyes, hearts that beat their last recurring rhythm too soon.

I can't breathe, as if my head has been thrust underwater. All the oxygen escapes my lungs and flies away. My throat is constricting.

A shadow appears over the village of corpses. I gaze at the figure. A woman with silver hair and a cloak like Death's, fresh blood marring her appearance. She stares at me. She smirks enigmatically. Turning sharply on her heel, she dashes away, into the shadows of the village. I pursue her, determined to not let her get away. She starts heading towards the hill with the fence. Does she know about it? Or is she just mindlessly fleeing? The woman flings the gate open, and the sky hisses. It starts sobbing and screaming, shouting and snivelling. The holes in the sky are burning open faster than they ever have.

I'm catching up to this inscrutable woman. She stops abruptly. I look past her to see why she has.

A hole. Like the ones in the sky, but down here. Like a portal... The rip in the atmosphere roars.

"Follow me if you want. I know you want to leave here."
The woman glances back at me. "But why? Why did you kill them?"
She ignores me. "So, will you stay here and go into negative amounts of sanity, or will you follow my lead?"
"What will happen if I follow you?"
She grins, sly and cryptic. "So, so much, little girl. You will trigger centuries of confusion and catastrophes. Your name will stain the history books until society cracks and crumbles to dust. Schoolchildren will revere you for what you'll have done, or abhor you for how much you'll increase their workload."
She offers me her hand. Without a second thought, I take it. She leads me through the portal. We step into a large room, filled with people.
I don't look back. They look at me, sudden hope exploding in their eyes. When they speak, their voices are full of unwavering colour. "Welcome, Empress Anastasia."

Zoe Difford (13)
Bodmin College, Bodmin

Kidnapped!

My name is Sophie Winter, I remember the day I was
kidnapped on 18th of December 2016, I was 11 years old.
As I went for a walk through the forest with my dog I was
walking but behind me was a dodgy man dressed in all
black dressed suspiciously. As I was near the end the man
tapped me on the shoulder asking if he could stroke my dog
so I said yeah. (My dog has a collar that says my mum's
number and our address if he went missing.) He said, "Can I
take a photo of your dog 'cause it's cute and I'm thinking of
getting one of these breeds?"
I said, "Yeah why not," until noticed what he was doing, he
was taking a picture off her collar. I said, "Show me your
phone, I know what you're up to!"
He said, "Why?"
So I said, "Just show me."
So he passed me his phone and I deleted it.
I got to the end of the forest and there was a car with
blacked-out windows and 5 men came out of the car and
the man that took the photo was there as well behind,
laughing as they dragged my dog off me (Trixy). I started
screaming in fear while one of the men covered my mouth
with an old rag and another man taped my feet and arms
together
As they chucked me in the boot I could hear them
tormenting my dog by
hurting it. My heart was pounding, I was crying in fear. All I
wanted was my dog and I wanted to go home.

I fell asleep in the back of the car and as I woke up I was getting dragged out of the car in the middle of some fields. One of the men said, "We can either kill you and take your dog back home or kill the dog and take you home."
I said, "Me," and as he pulled the gun out of the car and got the rope taken off me I remembered I had a pair of scissors. So as he held the gun towards my head I got my scissors out and stabbed him. I grabbed the gun off him shot all of his other friends. After that, I got the car keys and got my dog and drove off and eventually got home, but that's not the end of it.
Remember me saying about the photo that he took of my dog's collar with my address on it? Somehow he got it back and burned my house down and killed me, my mom, my dad, my dog and my 2 siblings. He soon got found and got put in jail for 9 years.

Lola Guest (12)
Chaucer School, Sheffield

14

The End

This is the end. The birth of me was the starting point. During it all, ridiculed by others... Then it came into play, the secret was out. We always hated what I was. Everyone finding out made it worse. I know this for sure.
They are almost here.

To whoever is reading my final words, burn my hanging body. Burn it and every piece of evidence to show I existed. Like we wrote, this is the end. I know what I am. Creatures like me shouldn't exist. You are human, but you shouldn't exist either... Should you friend?
Wake up...

Rhianna Baines (14)

Dereham Neatherd High School, Dereham

A Teenage Hurricane

It's a storm, a crash
A spiral tornado
A drop of rain is now a storm
A day of sun is only a drop of happiness
This is how teenagers feel...
Watch out for puberty
It's a hurricane and explosion in one!

Rhiannon Kendra Diane Nethercote (15)
Dereham Neatherd High School, Dereham

Dragon

Oh mighty creature of the past
I hear your timeless voice at last,
you've been a legend for too long
in fairy tale and ancient song.

You are a myth, an honoured beast,
the long-gone folk in your name did feast.
On golden tapestries they've sewn,
your shining form they carved in stone
your ice-cold gaze, your talons sharp
but never showed your breaking heart.

Now from the page upward you fly
with emerald scales and silver eye
shining in the pale moonlight
through clouds of blue-green butterflies
For ever on and on you fly
I guess that this must be goodbye.

Fare thy well oh magic one,
that dragon who I kept too long.
I kept you to myself
inside the book upon my shelf,
but now I set you free.

You must take flight
and be the one who brings the light.

Oh dragon of the endless past,
I've let you go, you're real at last.

Scarlett Moon (13)

Drumduan School, Forres

Why?

I thought about it for a while:
Did you enjoy hurting me?
Did you get some satisfaction,
making me feel the way you did?
The real question is why?
Why did you feel the need to treat me that way?
Why did you do that to me?

But even after you tried to ruin the happiness and joy
in my life,
I was still able to find it.
And you might ask how I did it...
Well, I got parents to guide me,
and protect me from the bad.
Brothers to run around, and laugh with.
Friends.
They brought me happiness,
they brought me joy.
Actually, scratch that,
they *are* my joy, they *are* my happiness!
No matter what you said to me to hurt me.
I still had them by my side.

And no, that doesn't mean I haven't been hurt badly
in my life,
or I haven't felt like I wasn't enough.

Because if I said to you
I haven't felt that way,
I would be lying.
And maybe for a while,
I felt that way,
but it's okay.
Because I have people who make me happy,
people who bring me to life.
I have people who put a smile on my face every day,
I have people who care about me.

The people I care about - maybe a bit too much about -
they care about me too,
but I'll always love them more.
I might never know why you hurt me
but in a way I thank you
because thanks to you I'm stronger.
And I protect myself with love,
through the people I love.

Moira Combe (14)
Drumduan School, Forres

Charlotte Corday's Diary, Last Entries

I am a proud republican, I believe in liberty, freedom and humanity. I hate Marat, he has betrayed the ideals of the revolution. Marat has diminished the ideals of the revolution. Marat kills innocent people every day, even children. I detest him! The violence and bloodshed makes my blood boil; this is why I killed him.

I have been sent to the guillotine for killing the monster man Marat, I stabbed him in cold blood. He was in his bath soothing his skin rashes when... I walked into his bedroom and began talking of the conspiracy, when I showed him a letter and concealed in the envelope was a knife and then, while he was soothing his rashes, I impaled the knife into his stomach. His arms flailed, in an attempt to haul himself out of the bath, but all in vain. Over his agonising screams, I sang the La Marseillaise. When Marat gave his final shriek the guards came and took me away.

I never told my mother or father what I was about to do, and now I can't even say goodbye. I am angry yet at peace. I know I've done what is right and now I will go to heaven with a clean conscience.

I wish I could speak to my fellow French people, but like so many others they will just play the big drums over me and then, I will be gone just in a second, insignificant, unimportant, worthless, alone, alone in a world which does not want me, does not need, does not know me... I wish I could just go, blow away in the wind, and be free, but my life binds me, but it won't be long.

I have just written a letter to my parents and said what I had to say, I cried and wept thinking of the time we could have had, then I stopped. I heard the sound of the drums and then slice, some poor soul had just been killed and then my heart fluttered, knowing I would be next.

Now the guard has arrived. He stood right in front of me and said these are your last moments, enjoy them. I thought, bring it on, let the blade come down on top of me and slice my neck and bring my end to this worthless land of mental foe. So I said to the guard, "You're in my way!" Elbowing past him, I made my way through the dungeon, I strode to the guillotine, knelt down to write these last few lines. I will sign off now and cast this letter to the crowd. Goodbye xxx

The late Charlotte Corday
RIP End of diary
P.S. God bless our world and save it for me from its unworthy foes.

Alexander Mills (15)
Drumduan School, Forres

I Am Not Who You Think I Am

I am not who you think I am.
Well, that depends.
Who *do* you think I am?
I don't know you, but let me guess.

Do you think, as I think you do,
That I am one of those people,
The ones we have all seen?
The brainwashed ones,
The mindless ones,
Who might be *smart*,
But cannot really think?

Do you think, as I think you do,
That I will grow to fit these walls, these rules,
That everyone has given me?
Well,
I hope not *everyone*.

I hope there are some people,
Who will not give me walls *nor* rules.

Do you think, as I think you do,
That I will live like everyone else I see,
Everyone *you* see?
Is that truly what you think?

Is it?
Honestly?

Do you think, as I think you do,
That when I am older and wiser, as they say,
I will be like you?
Like you expect me to be?
Really?

You might *think* you know me,
But you don't know me at all.

Do you think, as I think you do,
That when I grow up I will work for you,
Do what you say?
Maybe, *maybe* you think,
You will tell me what to do.

Do you think, as I think you do,
That besides commanding me,
You will tell me how to live?
How to feel?
Why?
What could you really, *possibly*,
Hope to gain?

I don't want that.
I am *not* who you think I am!

Please,
Understand,
None of that is *me!*
I am not who you think I am!

Do you think, as I think you do,
That I love this and I hate that,
Everything you expect of me?
No.
Even if you think otherwise,
None of it is true.
Not *ever*.

Do you think, as I think you do,
That you know what I think,
And what I know?
Not once.
You can act with all the swagger that you want.
You may *never* know what I think.
Or what I know.

You can lie all you wish.
None of it is true.

Do you think, as I think you do,
That you,
Know me?
No.

Not even *you*,
Could think up such a fantasy.

Do you think, as I think you do,
That I do not understand or worse,
That I do not feel?
Say what you like.
Fill the heads of those you love with *lies!*
I do understand.
And as I do understand,
I feel.

I *feel.*
I dream, I wish, I think, I strive, I hope.

Do you think, as I think you do,
That I have never seen the light of day,
Or better yet, the truth?
Well, I have.
I *have* seen the light of day,
The night,
The dark,
The truth.

Do you think, as I think you do,
That I am so gullible as to believe,
The lies that you will tell me?
For the last time,
No!

No, a thousand times!
Again, again, *again!*
How many times do I have to tell you?
I am not who you would force me to be!
I am not who you think I am!

I am everything the world wants me to be.
I am all *I* want to be.

I am every single thing which you,
Would suppress.
Everything you hate.
All that you despise.

I am everything that you do not want me to be.

My name?
I won't tell you.
What I will tell you is this -

I am me.

I am not who you think I am.

Isabella Davidson (13)
Drumduan School, Forres

Reunion Story

Me and my son Jake were in the car on our way to launch the speed boat we'd just made. It was a long drive to the harbour and when we got there Jake was already half asleep, after a 6am rise. We launched the boat and it floated so we got our stuff together and packed it all into neat piles in the boat. I then helped Jake into the boat and drove out of the harbour. The water was nice and calm and we were just starting to eat our lunch when we felt the boat lurch violently from side to side. We looked up to find a raging tornado coming straight towards us. "Mayday Mayday!" I screamed through the radio but there was no answer; *boom!* The tornado hit us. The boat got split in half and I saw Jake's hand disappear into the murky water. The glass from the windscreen smashed on my head knocking me out cold.

When I came around I was cold and wet, my first thought was: *is Jake safe?* "Jake, Jaake, Jaaaaake," I screamed but there was no answer. A deep sense of dread, sorrow and anger soon came across me. I saw two bright lights coming towards me.

When the lights came closer I could see that it was an RNLI lifeboat. It stopped a little way off and lowered its RIB, which came over and took me to the lifeboat. I kept asking if they knew where Jake was, but the answer was the same every time. No. I jumped up and rushed to the side of the boat. I was about to jump off to look for Jake but the coastguard men came and stopped me.

15 years later

I was driving along in my blue Rolls Royce Silver Shadow when I spotted a drive-thru car wash. My car was a bit dirty so I decided to give it a wash. I drove into the car wash and as soon as I had stopped the car I heard a faint buzzing sound as the car wash entrance and exit sealed up. I was trapped, no way out and no way in. The buzzing became louder and louder until it was a slow deep bone crushing drone. Suddenly I felt my stomach leap as the car wash jolted up. I went so far upwards it got hard to breathe and all I could see was black.

When I opened my eyes I could see that I was chained to a metal board, with a sheet of glass in front of me which meant I could see the dark blue circle of a planet which we were plummeting towards and we showed no signs of slowing. We were now minutes away from hitting the planet and as we got closer I could see the whole planet was covered in water. Suddenly, *bang!* We hit the water.

The sea was a lovely turquoise with coral reefs of pink, gold, green and every colour you could think of. I could see we were approaching a cave. We went into it and the car wash grew legs and landed on a rock. Three men came into my compartment and unchained me from the board:

"Aaarrggh!" I screamed.

The men weren't ordinary men. They had feet that looked like an ordinary man's hand which had no thumb. Their legs were as long as a normal man's calf. Their bodies were as long as a normal man's arm. They had no arms. Their hands were as big as a normal man's foot. Their heads were as big as a golf ball and their eyes were as small as pin holes.

"Who are you?" I said angrily.

"Gobbledygooks," they snapped back.

The Gobbledygooks led me to the door which had just appeared. They went to open it. "Noooo!" I screamed, but they just ignored me. They opened the door and I thought I would drown, but I didn't. I could see the water at the mouth of the cave but it wasn't coming in. The Gobbledygooks led me further into the cave. We eventually came to a clearing where I saw lots more of the Gobbledygooks. In the centre of them there was a big box with no windows. "What's in there?" I asked.

"You'll find out in good time," they said, "but first you must prove you're worthy of knowing. You will be put to work in the meantime."

2 months later

"Please, I've been working so hard. I ask for the 15th time *what's in the box?*" The Gobbledygooks were taken by surprise. "Fine," they said, walking to the door to open it. "Jake," I whispered to myself. "Jaaaaake!" I screamed. "Daadddd!" Jake screamed back. We ran forwards and hugged. I said, "Come on, let's get out of here." But Jake said, "Dad wait! The Gobbledygooks are just lonely."

"Oh okay," I said, "why don't we go back to Earth and make our Rolls Royce able to travel between Earth and here?"

"Okay," said the Gobbledygooks.

Jake and I eventually finished the Rolls Royce and spent Christmas with the Gobbledygooks.

William Slater (13)

Drumduan School, Forres

Power Of Poetry

I find a comfortable chair
Blank paper in front of me
Fingers poised with a pen
Patiently waiting to record my thoughts
My brain is like a match ready to ignite
Waiting for the moment when...
Boom
An idea pops into my mind
Sentences form in my brain
Rush through to my fingertips
Words flow like paint onto a canvas
A volcano erupting with lava
Gushing erratically yet somehow forming delicately
One word, two, three, sentence
Rhyming couplets then a verse
One verse, two, three, a page
Without much conscious thought or deliberation
Spontaneous and free
Like waves crashing on the shore
Creativity that welled up from nowhere
Love, loss, inspiration, and so much more
Passion and personal interpretation
I come to my last few lines
Oh, the power of poetry
My balance is restored.

Pearl Hara Yamazaki (12)
International School Of The Sacred Heart, Tokyo

Life Chapters

When I was one year old
Life was easy and everything was controlled
I loved the stars, the moon, and the sun
And all wanted was to have constant fun

Two years old, loved to play around
Travelling with my grandma, all over town
Both of our hands overlapping together
Deeply hoping it would last forever

The following year, I made it to three
Walking, running, and chatting so free
I made a best friend in my little kindergarten
Everything was perfect, never to be forgotten

Four years old, I would laugh at home
TV was my favourite and so was Mom
I sang songs really loud and totally off tune
Like a wolf howling to a full moon

Very soon, I was five years old
I turned to my best friend, who I then told...
"We're always going to be best friends, nothing can stop us"
We swapped some items and made a little fuss

Six years old, in a new school
First knew no one, I felt like a fool

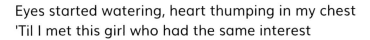

Eyes started watering, heart thumping in my chest
'Til I met this girl who had the same interest

Seven years old, indeed loved school
Learned to tie shoe laces, which was super cool
Jump rope was my ideal sport
Even though was relatively short

Eight years old, now a third grader
Exploring anything 'n' everything like a tomb raider
Excited to grow older day by day
And to see all the high schoolers in the hallway

Nine years old, finally in grade four
Everything was going well that was for sure
Reading, writing and learning so many things
Enjoying each day and everything it brings

Another year came, and finally turned ten
Still no problems, nice and peaceful again
Social media became more of an interest
An outlet for times when I felt a little stressed

Eleven years old and things started to change
Feeling left out, moving parts did rearrange
I locked my feelings and kept them very private
I wanted to cry but could not tell a classmate

Twelve years old, things became much worse
Some friends left me, like I had a curse

I tried to be nice, tried to be kind
Life was becoming more complex did find

Almost thirteen, another year gone
Still feeling like a bit of a black swan
One day I am up and the next I am down
But try my best to keep my feet on the ground

I think that life is like a special fairy tale
But much longer and with more intricate detail
New chapters are formed with each passing age
And are presented with each turn of the page...

Yena Lee

International School Of The Sacred Heart, Tokyo

Heartbeat

Beeping machine next to a hospital bed
A feeble patient lying unconscious
Eyelids closed on a pale face
Not a finger in motion

Beep, beep, beep, beep

Is this what nothingness is?
The departure from this Earth?
One heartbeat at a time
Coming closer to the tragic end?

Beep, beep, beep, beep

Worried relatives praying
Doctors and nurses frantically running around
Yelling demands flowing through the room
Crying parents and children.

Beep, beep, beep, beep

Yet in this mad chaos
The stillness and nothingness doesn't fade away
Only the sound of a beeping machine
To know a life is still here.

Roma Hara Yamazaki (12)
International School Of The Sacred Heart, Tokyo

One Week Of The Year

It is mental health week,
Where people with mental illness can speak.
It is the one week of the year,
Where others should lend an ear.

We need to open our eyes,
Listen for those silent cries,
Be a strong advocate and beacon of hope,
Help when people cannot cope.

They may recognise what we go through,
There is some hope that they do.
Maybe then people can better understand,
That there is a major problem at hand.

Reach out a helping hand,
Try, try, try to understand.
Share a smile and a caring word,
Don't be ashamed to let your voice be heard.

1 in 4 people have issues with their mental health,
Irrespective of their status and/or personal wealth.
Mental illness does not and will not discriminate,
And so too, it is not determined by fate.

We need to open our eyes,
Listen for those silent cries,

Be a strong advocate and beacon of hope,
Help when people cannot cope.

Let's reduce the stigma,
Mental health is not an enigma.
It can happen to any single one of us,
Let's seek help and make a fuss.

Reach out a helping hand,
Try, try, try to understand.
Share a smile and a caring word,
Don't be ashamed to let your voice be heard.

It is unacceptable in this day and age,
That we ignore and don't engage.
And talk about what is not necessarily in sight,
But we know, deep down, to be right.

We need to open our eyes,
Listen for those silent cries,
Be a strong advocate and beacon of hope,
Help when people cannot cope.

Don't just listen for a day or a week,
Listen when anyone chooses to speak.
Of their ups and downs and daily despair,
Show your humanity and don't just stare.

Reach out a helping hand,
Try, try, try to understand.

Share a smile and a caring word,
Don't be ashamed to let your voice be heard.

Speak words of comfort,
Let's make the effort.
Help those who are struggling with mental strife
Lead a happy, healthier and more positive life.

Aya Nassar (15)
International School Of The Sacred Heart, Tokyo

A Survivor

I am a bird
A lost bird roaming the night
As the day grows longer
There is no way to stay out of sight
I feel the breeze under my feathers
Becoming colder and colder
I brace myself
Seeking nothing but comfort
I am an outsider
An intruder
A survivor
I was revealed to the outside world
As I flapped my weak wings
Resting weary and fragile
Incapable of singing
Incapable of crying
Feeling broken
Thrown away
Not human
A monster
A disgrace
It is always the *us* and *them*
Who is the *real* monster
And here I stand under a spotlight of sorrow
Persevering through a path dark and narrow
People around me fell

Miserably destroyed
I am not going to fall
No matter how many times they knock me down
I will find my way
I am going to break through this cage
One day, my spirit will soar.

Grace Su (14)
International School Of The Sacred Heart, Tokyo

With No Voice

There are days we feel as though we are voiceless
We are trapped by situations that make us numb
The way I feel as if I am trapped
Like my mouth is sealed shut
The words are dead silent
As if I am not human...

I speak with boldness but silence is all we hear
With no voice
Who will listen?

Stuck in a box with the world against you
The world is quiet with no one to listen
Anger is shoved beneath us
With no right to speak
People with voices loud and strong
Our voice silenced as if we are dead

Lost in our silence
With no one to listen
When our voice is silenced
Then what is our purpose?

Our words that are silent
As if I am wrong
The people I can hear with booming voices
But I am not one of them
Then who am I?

My words are silent
As if I am not human
With no voice
Who will listen?
Then who am I without a voice?

Ayana Bessho (13)

International School Of The Sacred Heart, Tokyo

Feuer

Pungent smell of bellicose sweat
Furnishes the menacing atmosphere
As each star ignites
Immersed in the animated scarlet claws
Every single fibre gashed to the core
Shrill laughter of the hot-blooded soldiers
Echoes in our frail minds
Creating an everlasting concussion
That leaves us tremoring and unsettled
Stench of acrid cigarettes
Unequivocally present
How long will it take for them to recognise their sins?
Forcing the cumbersome burden
Of our motherland's losses
On our virgin shoulders
Imprinting our innocent minds
With abiding terror
Mouths agape
Lips encrusted from dehydration
Rancid carrions scattered all over
Compelled to wrap themselves around the inferno
Composing a cacophony only the devil savours
Like snakes angling for mice
Daggers had lacerated through the robust ties of affiliation
And as each thread veined

It marked the beginning of this discord
Of ravaging crimson.

Rena Tabuchi (13)
International School Of The Sacred Heart, Tokyo

A Fantastical Story

The smell of fresh books
The scent of freshly printed paper makes me want to read
And with one page the adventure begins
Propelled into a fantastical story
I ask myself, what will it be today?
A fight between a goblin and a fairy?
A wicked witch and a handsome prince?
The sun beams through my bedroom window
Brightens my page and my heart
I can escape into a fictional world of possibilities
I am a heroine ready to defend my kingdom
Fighting dragons, wizards and other mythical creatures
Casting spells, mixing potions, slaying dragons, riding a phoenix
Singing sweetly, floating through the air, speaking elfish, kissing a toad
Escaping from danger, riding gallant horses, sprinkling magic dust
I am the protagonist, then the antagonist
Just about to save the world when someone pushes me off a cliff
Hanging on by my fingernails
Page turn...
Propelled into a fantastical story
I ask myself, what will happen today?

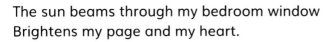

The sun beams through my bedroom window
Brightens my page and my heart.

Ashmi Kumar (12)
International School Of The Sacred Heart, Tokyo

The Winter Of 1941

The air was sharp and frigid
What used to be beautiful - green fields and blue skies -
now smoke-filled
The smoke smelly, sickly and thick
Odour of decimation and decay... of corruption and filth
Ahead, silhouettes of riots on the streets
Echoes of screams from petrified women and children
Men attempting to protect them, but all shot to death
Blood, guts and bones of dead bodies in decay lay strewn
about the devastation
Strewn over an acre of ground lay emancipated corpses
The horrible sight made me back away
Feeling a violent kick on my calf, I plummeted into the
remains of demolished buildings
I was thrown into a cattle car with so many others
Some vomiting and some lifeless
Knees scraped and bloodied
Arms covered with brightly coloured bruises
A thick, red fluid trickled down my fingertips
The bodies were finally thrown off the cattle car
Into the ground where people were rapidly losing blood
Countdown to my own imminent death
Losing vision; unable to look ahead
Everything disappeared and I started to see the delirium
of my mother...
Mama, I know you are not with me

And yet I feel you are here
Your warm arms embracing me
As the dust falls with the winter wind, so do my thoughts
fly away with you
I forget about the murders; the deaths
Because I believe that my dream will come true soon.

Alisa Pontes (14)
International School Of The Sacred Heart, Tokyo

Jallianwala Bagh

We met them without aggression
Yet they chose to teach a lesson

Soldiers with skin white as bone
Along with sepoys of our own

Their cruel eyes cut like a knife
Sucked us out of all our life

Amidst the heaps of bodies, I stood
Help them, I felt like I should

Yet I watched, numb, paralysed
As bullets pierced through their cries

A memory that I can't cut out
But I would love to live without

As the sun rose the next morning
I stood, sobbing, in mourning

The nauseating smell of bodies burning
And for my daughter I was yearning

Endlessly, night after night
I wonder if I'll ever feel alright

In my sleep, her face haunts me
Her screams ring, her dire pleas

In she jumped and down she fell
A long way down into the well

Bullet wounds stained the well's water red
As hungry kites circled overhead

Now although instead of blood
Flowers bloom, streaked with mud

Above toy kites with strings are flown
Surrounded by people yet I feel alone

The children live without a care
But I live with memories of the square

Myself I fear far more than guns
My thoughts I dread, the toxic ones

More harmful than a bullet ever was
Afraid of what my thoughts may cause

I'm left with my guilt, so severe
I'm left forever with my fear.

Namya Kumar (15)
International School Of The Sacred Heart, Tokyo

First Day Of School

Bzzt! Bzzt! Bzzt! The alarm went off at 6:30am and today was finally the day, a fresh start in a new school. I was trembling, quivering and shaking like a leaf. It was here. Now was the time. I told myself that I would be fine, it was my first day of school, a new book and a new life, but one day you were here every day of the week, playing with toys, reading books, hide-and-seek. Now those precious little legs have grown, I stay at home and go on my phone.

My parents always told me I was as precious as the day I was born, only that I'm not small. They said, "When did your limbs become so long? Once you were weak and now you are strong." Where does the time go from the moments we steal? I looked back at them now and they still felt so real. They waited at the gate for me. Once I went in there would be no coming back. I thought about my old friends from primary school, I wondered what they were doing and how Mr Reed is teaching the new year 6s.

Everything felt so different, I was in disbelief. We were taken to the playground where they showed us our new teachers and peers, but I didn't like it. I wanted to turn back time and just live to see another day in primary school.

All the teachers in my old school used to say, "Enjoy your time in here while it lasts." Now I realise how precious those moments were. I would do anything to get those moments back. The football every Thursday and the golden time when I would play board games with Louis and Luke gave me flashbacks to a happier time. Now I felt like crying. I now liked to say to myself, "We didn't know we were making memories; we were just having fun."

My new teacher walked my form to our new classroom and everyone sat down whilst I felt like leaving and running out of the door. I felt people giving me dirty looks from across the room and convinced myself that I wouldn't make any friends in this school, but I couldn't imagine having anyone as my friend apart from Louis and Luke anyway.

After form was over, my next lesson was maths. We sat in our assigned seats and the teacher handed out a new exercise book and a new pencil case to everyone. I wrote my name very carefully on the front cover and next opened my book and made no mistakes writing the date, title and margin because I didn't know how secondary teachers would act if you made a mistake. I always thought secondary school teachers were stricter than primary school teachers so that's why I did my best work. Back in primary, if you made a mistake the teacher wouldn't mind, and would just help you not make that mistake again.

As I was walking to my next lesson, I realised everyone was bigger than me but in year 6 we were the role models, the kings and queens of the school. We had a higher status than anyone else in any other year but now we were at the bottom. From hero to zero.

When the school day was over, I walked out thinking *this is only the beginning, I have another four to six years in this school.* Although I realised it was not all bad, I'd get used to it and everything happens for a reason. So maybe I am destined to be here.

Aron Matranxhi (13)
King Henry School, Erith

Best Birthday Ever

"Happy birthday to you, happy birthday to you, happy birthday dear daughter, happy birthday to you," sang Sidney's dad.

"Thanks Dad! The big one eight, I'm finally an adult." Like any normal teenager, Sidney has been dreaming about this day for years.

"Honey, put your birthday outfit on and meet me downstairs." Dad left her room and walked down the creaky stairs, and a few moments later Sidney followed. "Close your eyes Sidney it's a yummy surprise," Dad said while carrying a plate.

"Dad, I told you that I don't want to have my cake till the party," she spoke with a sweet tone.

"I know, I know, I'm not dumb! Speaking of the party, who's coming again? Anyone I don't like?" he laughed while still holding the plate and forgetting that Sidney still had her eyes closed.

"Dad, can we do this in a minute, I wanna know what you're holding. I smell syrup, is it pancakes?" she said licking her lips.

"Sidney, why do you know everything?" he said with a groan.

"Does that mean I can open my eyes and eat some yummy pancakes?" She opened her eyes and took the plate and gave Dad a hug.

Sidney gobbled down the pancakes. "Just like Mum use to make them." A tear dropped from his eye.

"Dad, it's my birthday, I can't be sad on my birthday! Remember, Mum always used to say that," she said with a smile on her face.

"Okay back to what I wanted to know, who is coming to this party?" Dad said, wiping away his tears.

Trying to distract her dad from thinking about her mum, who had died suddenly of a heart attack when she was only three, Sidney listed as many people she could think of.

"Okay so Amy, Anisha, Bethany, Chantel, Charlie, Danny, Eli, Ellie, Ella, Freddy, Georgina, Isabella, Katy, Maisy, Max, Rosie and I don't know for certain, but Sophia might be coming, is that alright Dad?" she coughed as if she was rapping.

"Sidney that's like sixteen/seventeen people! How many are over 18, because I ain't looking after that many children." Although he loved his daughter, he was struggling to raise her since losing his wife. He did not have someone to go to when he was stressed or annoyed but as Sidney got older, she understood her dad more and developed a bond with him. You know the saying 'like father like son', well they are the opposite, 'like father like daughter.'

"Dad only Katy is 17 but she turns 18 next month and is very mature. Please tell me that's alright?" Sidney glared at her dad with sympathetic eyes.

"Oh, how can I say no to you, you're my star," he said with the biggest smile on his face.

At around lunchtime, Sidney left home to go and do some birthday shopping with some of her best friends, so that they could get some cute outfits for the party. Between them they had 100 to spend on hair, make-up and clothes. When they arrived at the shopping mall, they went down to the food court. For lunch, she had her most favourite meal, chicken nuggets from McDonald's. She and her friends wandered through the shopping centre for almost five hours.

By the time she got home people had already started showing up for the party. "Katy of course you're the first one here! Who dropped you off? The party starts at six! Want to come upstairs and get ready with me?" Sidney said, holding her dress.

"No one dropped me off, your dad needed help so he gave me a call and I walked here. I only live around the block and I will get dressed in a bit we still need to set up outside." Sidney went upstairs and decided to write a quick note in her diary before the party. 'Dear diary, it is exactly a year since I began writing these documentations of my life. I'm 18 now, that's so cool! Today I bought one of the prettiest dresses that I have ever seen I think, my dad will love it! Bye bye, don't die.'

Sidney put on her dress and when she finished, everyone came to the bottom of the stairs. Their eyes went straight to her dress. It was poofy and the glitter glimmered against the party lights. They partied and partied till 10 that night and then her dad brought out the cake. Two layers of vanilla and red velvet with the big one eight on top.

"Sidney, it's cake time," her dad said with a big grin on his face as everyone sang happy birthday. Sidney blew out the candles and wished for this day to never end.

"To my wonderful daughter, I have loved you from the day I set eyes on you." A teardrop fell from his eye and Sidney knew it came from his heart. After the cake had been gobbled down, the party continued for another hour or so before it was gift time.

"Everyone, it's gift time," bellowed Sidney. She went through every gift and while she loved every single one of them, she noticed that her dad did not have a present for her.

55

"Sweetie, close your eyes I'm going to go and get your present from me." He walked off and came back with a box. "Sweetie open your eyes." He handed her the heavy box. Sidney opened the box and out jumped a puppy.
"OMG Dad a puppy!" she squealed.
"That's not all sweetie, look at the collar," he said with a big smile.
"Dad no, that's a pair of keys to a Range Rover," she said, confused. "They're yours! I love you Sidney," he smiled.
"Dad, I love you too," as a tear fell from her eye.

Lucia Grilli (12)
King Henry School, Erith

My Way Of Life

Only 30 seconds left until the bomb explodes. I am a special force member running through the streets and killing terrorists, I had to defuse the bomb that terrorists loaded in the centre of our town.

It looked like it had only 10 seconds left, I was running, running and running but the terrorists seemed to have resurrected. 3, 2, 1 and I thought it was too late! I went to the bomb because nothing seemed to happen, I looked around and saw my friend, Joe Selkman, who was trying to cut an electricity charger in the bomb. *Cut!* He looked at me with a happy face. "Nick! Did you do well?"

I looked at him as well and answered, "Yes of course, I was trying to defuse the bomb as well but I see you did it faster." We chatted for a few minutes and went out of the town centre where we were greeted by citizens.

The next day I had a strange feeling, it must have been the stress from the day before but it wasn't, I thought for over ten minutes and realised that I wanted to be the same as Joe Selkman.

On my way to the military base, I saw some outlaws and that's when I thought my job would start again. I ran as fast as a cheetah to call other special force members but no one was around so I thought I had to do it myself. The outlaws were trying to switch a mega bomb on, this time it had only 10 seconds.

Without the correct tools, I took myself in hand and as a shadow crawled to the outlaws then using my jujutsu skills rushed and slammed the outlaws and in the time when they were scared I banged their heads together and knocked them out and defused the bomb.

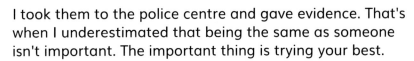

I took them to the police centre and gave evidence. That's when I underestimated that being the same as someone isn't important. The important thing is trying your best.

German Pankov (12)
Lockers Park School, Hemel Hempstead

Signing

I feel honoured to be signing in assemblies.
I am happy to be able to do sign language.
I can smell the equipment in the room.
The room looked like an office.
I am thinking about being a Makaton teacher.
I first started signing when I was in primary school
One of my old TAs taught me how to sign using Makaton and BSL.
I felt excited and so happy to be able to sign in assemblies and at home.
Using Makaton is easy to learn
But we all need to take baby steps, one at a time!
When I was ten I had a baby face,
Also it was my first time doing signing and it was amazing.
I used to watch Liz signing in assembly!

Grace Turner (16)
Marjorie McClure School, Chislehurst

It'll End Soon...

As I gasp for breath my lungs fill with the poisonous gas lingering around this cell, blood splatters on the walls. I'm afraid and I don't know what to do. I have lost all hope in life. All I do now is wait to die.

I stand in chains, my ankles being sliced by the hard metal, my blood seeping through the cracks in the individual pebbles covering the ground that stab my bare feet. We are no longer free. We are now the property of our government. Women are now only seen as being able to repopulate the demised Earth and those who aren't able or are too young are chained up and experimented on by psychopaths. As I do now, people wait in the worst conditions possible, hoping to make it out of this hell alive. We are like their dummies, dummies that are carelessly dumped in wretched rooms and put through the worst agony imaginable, each time being subjected to the games, losing faith in the process. They experiment on us to see how a certain gas or drug affects the body.

I am surprised that even though I have been plagued with so many experiments, I am still alive with only some red boils located on my neck to show for it.

I freeze as a nefarious 'scientist' looks into my acrimonious eyes and whispers, "You next."

I walk through the yellow hallway, my knees in agony, my head in turmoil, my arms violently shaking. I am stupefied. My heart is racing and my lungs feel like they are going to collapse. Lunatics in white coats stand in the long maze of a corridor showing me the way.

A prodigious door opens in front of me. A scientist from inside the room seizes my arm and drags me in. There is a window showing the neighbouring room full of scrimpy scientists. There are air vents covering the ceiling and the room is full of other human guinea pigs but I feel isolated. A microphone from the other room squeaks. A female scientist says, "Close the vents and door to begin the experiment."

I hear the vents snap more accelerated than lightning. My heart skips a beat. I hear the pernicious gas being pumped into the room. I try to hold my breath but my lungs can't stand it anymore, I have to inhale. Abhorrent minutes pass, feeling like hours. The room fills with daunting screams that echo off the walls.

A woman no older than twenty grabs my arm for balance. As she falls she howls in pain, her eyes a devilish black. Champange-coloured blood drips from her nose and ears. Terror shines from her face. Her hands lose grip and she collapses onto the floor, blood pouring like a river from her mouth. She screams a wild scream and then dies a horrific death. Many people drop like flies, screaming flies covered in bloody faces, displaying agony, and I am waiting for death to take me; because of the horrors I've experienced, I would go gladly.

Time passes sluggishly. Screams in my head are bouncing off the padded walls. I can see the scientists waiting patiently without a conscience or any guilt on their immoral faces. I finally can only hear one scream, a piercing scream. I turn around to make eye contact with the only other person in the room to give them comfort.

My face drops as I see them, they are a young girl no older than six years of age, tears streaming from her eyes, her clothes covered in other people's blood and sorrow. I run to her, hoping to hug her to give her a feeling of comfort. I step over the dead victim's body and my feet squelch in the pools of blood. I grab her and hold her in my arms. Her innocent eyes stare helplessly at me. She plucks up the strength and whispers, "Help me." My heart shatters as someone so young, someone who never harmed anyone in her short life, has to be subjected to these grim experiments.

I am alone in this blood-splattered, stinking room, scientists monitoring my every move. I just stand here waiting to die. I hear the dreaded microphone squeal and a male scientist says, "Don't worry, it'll end soon."

Caitlin McAlpine (13)

NCEA Duke's Secondary School, Ashington

The Runaway

Chapter 1: Iaino

Thunder crashed.

"Huh," groaned William. "W-w...where am I?" William said.

A deep groan of a creature echoed through the forest.

"W-W-W-W-WHAT WAS THAT?" he yelled.

A growl followed.

William ran through the forest as fast as he could but the figure followed, racing toward William as if it knew where he was going to go. And then he found a watch tower. He raced up it as fast as he could then when he reached the top it was dusk and it was too dark to make out what the thing was.

"What in the world is going on?" William shouted, trying to understand.

Then he started to see the light of a lantern glowing. But then it faded with a man wailing in the distance. It was terrifying knowing that it could have been him if he had been running in the dark. He realised that the creature was running under the shadows of the tree and that it could not be climbed.

Chapter 2: The Brink Of Dawn

At the brink of dawn, William started to run to the guy with the lantern to see if he survived but when he arrived it was horrific. The man was ripped to shreds and it wasn't by a creature of this world. Whatever it was it wasn't hunting for food, it was hunting for sport, slaughtering anything in its path no matter if it was the same species. It would not be easy to get rid of something that could hunt about twenty elephants in a minute.

William really didn't think it would have an ordinary weakness. Maybe the man had stuff for him to use. Another scream from the distance was followed by the roar of the alien creature. It wasn't too far away - it was hunting more and more humans but he might be next so he needed to get up high for the night. Maybe- "Ah, a lighthouse I could use for the night," William said, trying to hide the fact he was next.

Then the rain started to pour again. The sky started to move slowly.

He was running out of time. The creature was going to get him but he was so close. He ran as fast as he could, listening to the monster's heavy breathing and far-spread steps. As he opened the door of the lighthouse the creature ripped off his jacket with its needle-like claws. It started to claw at the door, tearing through the wood.

William mounted the ladders and rushed up them, barely getting past the blood-lusted creature. William found two lanterns and lit one, throwing it down the ladder to see the creature. It looked like a bear, wolf and lion mixed. It was terrifying. William sat there till the morning.

Chapter 3: Multiply

An echoing screeching cut through the air, waking William. "Huh?" William shouted, half asleep.

Another yelp of pain came from the bottom of the ladders. William peered down the ladders to see the creature sliding away from the sunlight but it had already clawed too much off the door and it had burned. Then it dropped to the ground, most likely fainted.

William slowly climbed down the ladder to check if it was faking. Well, it was not faking so he leapt down the ladder to see its face and it looked rough with a fluffy mane and its snout was like a bear's. It was mainly black with a few different colours.

But I can't just keep calling it the creature so I should name it... William thought. *Hmmmmmm,* he thought. *Ah, I should name it sabertooth after the ancient cat.*

The pulse slowly faded in the animal. But there was still wailing from afar but it didn't seem to be the same as this one. Then the sabertooth burst into a flame like a phoenix but without a rebirth, the ashes blew off into the wind.

Bradley Thomson (13)
NCEA Duke's Secondary School, Ashington

Jaeda

Think of a circle. That's the only analogy of my situation that works right now. A nice, smooth, pervasive, never-ending circle. Pervasive because circles are everywhere, no matter if you are looking for them or not, no matter if you want them to be there or really kind of hate them. Never-ending because, well, it always circles back around. And whether your circle can be split into quarters or eighths or a million tiny pieces, eventually you end up back where you started. You're stuck in the same slow rotation going round, round, round.

I hate circles.

I've had this feeling before. It isn't new, is what I can determine from behind a wall of nauseatingly harsh sensation. It's different in ways but not new. It can't be new ever again. I miss not knowing the feeling.

She is perfect, I think as I hold her body in my arms. Her hair, soft curls, grazing the pavement as it spreads out over the support my arm supplies. Brown skin still glowing, warm and real and radiant against my paleness. Her lips, I see as I lean closer, poised to break out into a smile, ready to make it all worth it in an instant, but the smile doesn't come. Her dark eyes lie behind smooth eyelids, not scrunched or creased, perfectly smooth. I am grateful for these eyelids stopping me having to look at empty darkness, when I am so used to seeing it full, burning with animation, infinite in its feeling. Jaeda is an eternal light source that can outlast any star. She is ethereal, my lovely Jaeda.

I stare at her, my own eyes burning in their sockets, not only sore from insomnia but itching with tears I refuse to shed because I refuse to mourn. Jaeda's jacket is a pale off-white, hazier than the sterile purity of true white, easier on the eye, pleasing. Angry crimson drowns the sweet tones of the fabric, stemming from her abdomen where she is ripped wide open. The tear is at an angle, careless. It's like leaking ink over writing, distressing, messy. Infuriating. My face burns.

She was ethereal. Now she is growing cold and sickly as I hold her. Her blood covers my hands, marking my shirt and arms. Jaeda stains me as she bleeds out, seeps into my skin and holds onto me. I feel it, any second now it will begin. It has to. I tighten my grip, bringing her closer to me, pressing my face into her hair.

I dread the moment that comes all too quickly: a presence, cold and distant, burning with a freezing intensity, materialises to my right. My jaw clenches painfully as if it can shut it out, as if I've ever been able to shut it out.

Most people call it a gift. It's a gift I do not want.

"Clark."

Aching, I lift my head. The sight of her dead in my arms isn't what finally makes me cry; it's the sight of her standing over me, unharmed, unreal, *uncaring*. They never pity me — not that I'd want that — and they never sympathise either.

Forgive me, my love, for thinking you'd be different, because now that my hope is crushed a fractal of my soul will always despise the sight of you.

Jaeda is not indifferent as those before her. She crouches to my level, lays her unbodied hand over her lacerated side and breathes deep as if she is able to smell the blood that suffocates me.

I've never seen one of them consider their body before, they don't usually latch on immediately. I am a last resort for many, but I am Jaeda's first. I've failed her.

"Yes, you have."

In the overload of feeling, I have forgotten the extent of the curse. The shared intimacy. Ironically, death binds us in a way we never even neared, forces closeness of an unimaginable degree. She knows this, she knows *me*, which is why she isn't hysterical. Thoughtful, my brain wearily supplies, or else she pushes the word forward. Our minds are now laced as our hands once were. She's considering what this means for her. It occurs to me that she's considering how she feels about me.

People change when they die. They don't love who they used to. I am the living, and I love Jaeda as I did yesterday, wholly.

"That's nice, Clark. But does it really matter if you love me when I'm dead in your lap? You speak of your inhabitants like they're insects, parasites feasting on every last bit of joy and hope. Is that what's to become of me? I turn into some butterfly you think is pretty but worthless?"

"Stop," I say. Jaeda knows she's cutting, knows I never speak to the voices out loud if I can help it. Until now she probably doubted my sincerity or my sanity. "It's not the same with you."

"No, it isn't." She's standing again, looking more at her own closed eyes than at mine. "Because I'm not an insect that will die after a couple of weeks. Death didn't do us part, my love, and I know you'll grow to hate me for it."

"Never." My voice is a sickly imitation, a ghost. "Jaeda-"
"Don't say my name like it burns! You hold my body and act like *you're* hurting? I'm not a painful memory, Clark, I'm still real. I'm still here with you! Stop acting like I'm just another voice in your head."

Jaeda frowns, and I am looking at what I knew I'd see once she returned to me: hatred. She is poisoned in death, my love now an insult, our intimacy a weapon.

A lot of them hate me, but I am shielded from their abhorrence because they never cared for me in life. They do not know me but as the tether of their demise. They never knew me as a lover.

Mia Stockton (17)
New College Pontefract, Pontefract

Hidden Truth

The noise of passing traffic filled First Street in Washington DC mixed with the smell of coffee dancing through the air like a graceful ballerina. A young girl strolled down the sidewalk humming a jolly tune under her breath. A gust of wind vigorously launched a group of leaves across the block. The girl pulled down her hat, bowed towards the wind and began to pick up pace towards her friend's house. A raindrop suddenly fell on her shoulder; that raindrop then turned into a generous downpour. She hastily darted into the entrance to the Library Of Congress.

It's good that this library was here so I could shelter from the rain, she thought happily. _You know what, maybe I'll stay here for a bit longer, a few minutes won't hurt._

The girl walked into the massive building to see a receptionist looking at her.

"Is there anything I can help you with?" the receptionist asked.

"I'm okay thanks," replied the girl.

Her phone suddenly began to ring loudly. She quickly hung up and continued to walk deeper into the library. She finally got to a nice part and sat down and began reading a copy of Little Women.

Hours passed without her even realising but then she abruptly realised about her arrangement to go to her friend's house, so the girl packed up her stuff and began to walk to where (she thought) the exit was. The last thing ever heard from the young girl that evening was a quiet gasp. Her phone and hat lay on the ground; the occasional message popping up including 'Where are you? This is the second time this week you are late, Constance!'

Constance woke up with an agonising headache and was sprawled across the cold, hard floor of the library but something wasn't right. She got up and looked out of the window to see loads of pedestrians wearing old suits and top hats.

"What the hell just happened?" Constance wondered as she steadied herself against a pillar.

"Can I help you young lady?" asked a man sitting at the front desk.

"This may be a weird question but what year is it?" asked Constance with a puzzled look on her face.

"Why, the year is 1800 of course, young lady," he replied with bemusement.

At his reply, Constance covered her mouth with shock and ran out onto the sidewalk to see a horse and cart passing by. She reached for her pocket and noticed her phone wasn't in it.

Why am I here, how did I get here and where is my phone? Constance thought as she paced back to the library, getting the occasional stare from other pedestrians due to her modern clothing.

She returned to the library and sat down where she began reading Little Women and suddenly felt a frigid feeling down her back. Constance looked behind her to see a floating and partially transparent boy looking at her. Constance screamed but no one heard her.

"Hello Constance," the boy muttered.

"How do you know my name?" Constance asked with a worried expression spread across her face.

"That doesn't matter, but what really matters is you. I brought you back to 1800 to tell you something important. During the construction of this library I was walking along and fell through the floorboards, landing in the foundations of the building, killing me and making me part of the structure."

"Why are you telling me this?" Constance asked curiously.

"Because you need to know, my death was covered up and now I am just an undiscovered body under the floor," replied the boy whilst looking down at the ground. "I want the truth to be known."

"How will I do that?" asked Constance.

"You will find a way," whispered the boy in her ear.

Constance suddenly felt a flush of warmth and the feeling of hitting the ground. She pulled herself onto her feet and looked around to see a few modernly dressed people browsing bookshelves.

I'm back! Constance thought as she remembered the boy and his disturbing message.

The girl ran over to reception to see a box labelled 'Lost and Found'. She looked inside to see her hat and phone and picked them up. Constance then walked over to the Little Women book she was reading before she got sent back in time and picked it up. She pulled out a piece of scrap paper from her pocket and fetched a pen from reception which was sitting on a 'Leave us a Review' sheet. Constance then wrote down what the boy had told her about his untimely death on the paper and slipped it in the back page of the book.

That should do it, she thought confidently before placing the book back on the shelf.

Constance then texted her friend saying, 'Sorry I'm late. On my way. Just had to pop a book back to the library. See you in five.'

Milo Durrant-Miller (11)

Penair School A Science College, St Clement

Crystal Of Universe

Dedicated to my caring mother and beloved late grandfather.

Iryna Shopska (short name - Ira) is a 36-year-old scientist and linguist, born in Kryvyi Rih, Ukraine. She knew her father (Volodymyr Orlov) as a scientist and a traveller, but unfortunately he died five years ago. It was a big trauma for my family. He was only 66. I can say my grandad was athletic and kind. Nevertheless, life goes on and we need to enjoy it.

The story...

Scientist, Iryna, was trying to invent a time machine in her garage for over three years and she was close to the end. Unfortunately, one part of her invention was missing and she couldn't find or create it, because this part contained rare chemical elements, that were only available to the government. However, one day whilst making her garden even more beautiful, Ira unearthed a corner of a small object in the ground. Further excavation resulted in the discovery of the black box with the two words: 'Volodymyr Orlov' (who was her late father). The excited scientist impatiently opened the box. There was a small item carefully wrapped in paper and photos of Iryna's family. Unbelievably, that item turned out to be the missing part of the time machine! After this godsend, Ira finally finished her creation!

Entering the machine, some voice asked for her full name. The scientist answered. A 3D projection of her father appeared and started to talk.

'Dear Iryna,

It's me, your father, Volodymyr Orlov. Congratulations, you've finished the time machine! When you were born I invented it. However, I knew I couldn't do a lot with it, so I disassembled it, left parts of it and short instructions in the garage. The very important detail was hidden in our garden, so only you could find it and complete the machine. I was always sure that my daughter had potential to be a great scientist or inventor. After I finished building the time machine, I travelled to the year 1892, Kryvyi Rih, Ukraine, to see how it was about a hundred years ago. I landed near an iron ore mine and went to explore it. Inside I found some abandoned minecarts and tools. Some very strange feelings prompted me to go back to the machine and return home. Before leaving, I glanced back at the depth of the mine and some extremely shiny thing caught my eye.

My time has run out and I can't stay with you forever and help. But I'll be watching you from above and send you luck, fortitude and happiness. Don't worry about me, we can meet if you return to year 1980 and enter our house, my soul will transfer to the body at that time and we can do everything together. Don't show this invention to people, keep it secret, because the world can go crazy if everybody starts using the time machine.

Love you! Your father, Volodymyr Orlov'.

Iryna was deeply touched. She spent about a minute collecting her thoughts. Trembling, the scientist pushed the buttons of Year 1892, Kryvyi Rih, Ukraine and pressed 'start'. The time machine tore off the ground for a couple of centimetres and disappeared in the air.

Travel into the past began. The moon and the sun changed each other with crazy speed. After a couple of minutes, the door of the time machine opened and Ira stepped outside. It was 1892. Everything looked similar to 2022. Iryna landed near the mine and went to explore it. Descending, she saw some sort of light, coming from the stone wall. The next moment Ira was holding a diamond-shaped mineral in her hands. With a bit of effort, she cracked a small piece of strange ore. It was very unusual, unearth material. Fractured lumps of mineral became an entire piece. The scientist was holding two exact stones. She had never seen a mysterious material like that one. Iryna knew that if she took it home, future and present would change, so the scientist marked this place on the map and went to the time machine.

Travel back to the present, 2022, was quite fast. When the door opened, Iryna was back at her garage. She was quite happy to be home after this journey. Without wasting any time, Ira got into her car and drove to the place marked on the map. Fortunately, nothing happened with either the mine or the minerals. Worryingly, Iryna took the stone, she had discovered earlier. Afterwards, the scientist came back to her laboratory and started researching it. When the sun hit the crystal, it began to glow orange, brown, blue and when it was placed in the dark it started glowing like a bright lantern. Having left the stone in a container under the shiny sunrays, Iryna went to the library to look through science books, but she couldn't find anything about a diamond-shaped mineral in them. When the scientist came back home, she noticed a puddle of fuel under the crystal.

Iryna wanted to check if the puddle was from the mineral or something else, so she sat close to the plastic box and started staring at the stone: petrol was coming from the mineral. The scientist wrote this observation in her notebook. She wanted to explore other features and abilities of the crystal: she put it between two nails wrapped in metal wire connected to an ammeter to check if the crystal could produce electricity. The arrow on the screen of the tool went up immediately after everything was connected together. This meant that the mineral produced electricity itself. The diamond-like crystal was so powerful that you could use it to solve the world's problems! Iryna went back to the machine and travelled to meet her father. After a conversation with her dad, Ira arrived back in 2022, she decided to go to the authorities and show them the crystal. Soon there was an announcement on social media, news and radio that Iryna Shopska had found a mineral that could solve most of the problems around the globe. Ira became very famous and a lot of people were thankful for this godsend.

Ivan Shopskyi (12)

Penrice Academy, St Austell

Mission Tales: The Creature From Blackwood Forest

Chapter 1: Isaac Chatterton

Isaac looked up from the table. He'd fallen asleep in the bar again. He checked Jeremy (his pet chameleon). Jeremy had also fallen asleep.

Isaac woke himself up, he had to focus on why he was here: look for someone giving quests. He was almost broke and needed someone to give him a job.

He looked to the most interesting character in the bar. A human (around the age of 35) sitting at a table with a flamethrower (this is quite normal in this world).

Isaac went to the man and asked if the man had any quests for him. The man looked up and said, "As a matter of fact, I do. What are your skills?"

"I have sonic hearing!" Isaac said enthusiastically. Isaac was a Bith, an alien with supernatural hearing.

"That'll help you a lot," the man said. "Have you ever heard the legend of Blackwood Forest?"

"No," Isaac said. "What is it?"

The man lowered his voice and said, "The Wendigo."

The entire bar went silent. There were many dangerous creatures in this universe, from giant rats to dragons, but one of the most dangerous creatures on Planet Earth was the Wendigo.

The scariest thing about the Wendigo is how little is known about it.

"I can handle a Wendigo!" Isaac said enthusiastically but quietly.

"Good, but it won't be easy. Far from it," he chuckled slightly. "May I give you some advice?"

"Sure!" Isaac said.

"If it finds you, stand still," he said this extremely seriously.

Chapter 2: The Washington Lodge

Isaac arrived on Planet Earth. He took the bus to Blackwood Forest. The snowy landscape gave Isaac a calm feeling, reminding him of Christmas. He checked on Jeremy and started the walk up the hill.

He got to a ski lift station and took the lift up the rest of the mountain.

At the top of the mountain was the Washington Lodge. The home of the Washingtons. It was believed they owned the Blackwood Mines, but then something happened and they left the lodge behind.

Isaac ran to the door and tried to open it, maybe the house had heating!

As Isaac went to open the door, his sonic hearing went off. He heard a deer scream in pain and a demonic high-pitched scream.

Isaac immediately went to run back to the ski lift but froze. Something was watching him.

Chapter 3: The Wendigo

Isaac slowly looked left into the forest and saw what the old man told him about. Long limbs with a resemblance to a humanoid structure. The creature got closer, one step at a time.

Isaac remembered what the old man said: "If it finds you, stand still."

Isaac held back his urge to scream and held completely still. The creature finally came into the light. The blood dripping from the creature's mouth was emphasised more by the inhuman teeth and sharp nails. The creature was also extremely slender as if it had been starved. Its eyes looked as if they were slightly pushed into its skull.

The creature stared at Isaac as if it couldn't see him.

A twig snapped in the distance. The Wendigo screamed and ran on all fours towards the origin of the sound.

Isaac took the chance and ran to the ski lift, ignoring the fact the Wendigo had screamed as soon as he started running.

Isaac made it to the lift and shut the doors. He sat down on the floor to check on Jeremy. Jeremy was also terrified.

Isaac looked at the window in the door and saw the Wendigo was there, staring inside the lift. The Wendigo's attention immediately went to Isaac. But he was holding still! He looked down. His chameleon wasn't holding still. The Wendigo raised its arm and smashed through the window.

Isaac ran to the other end of the lift and watched as the Wendigo crawled through the window and looked right at him.

Chapter 4: Isaac Chatterton

The radio turned on: "*Breaking news!* Fear has risen in residents since the discovery of Isaac Chatterton's body. He was found dead in the ski lift in Blackwood Forest.

Detectives stated: "The body was found without a jaw, it seems to have been torn off with great speed. There was also the tail of a chameleon in the lift'. Many people are still trying to solve this mystery, but for now, Isaac Chatterton's death stays a mystery"."

Keanu Antonio-Scales (13)

Penrice Academy, St Austell

Purple

In a faraway village, there was a deep forest, a forest that was surrounded by a mysterious purple fog. Although no one had ever lived in this forest, those who would enter it would hear a beautiful voice singing in the wind. Attracted to it, many had entered this mysterious forest, but no one had ever returned. This forest was thus named the Purple Forest and since these incidents, no mere mortal would dare to enter this area, especially if they were alone. This is the tale of how one passing traveller attempted to free the town from its strife. But would she succeed?

Vesper Dawn continued to run, breath hitching in her throat. Darkness filled the sky, the forest engulfed in indigo fog. She heard a lonesome cry of a bluebird, before it suddenly screeched to a stop. Shivering, she turned, tracking the sound, only to hear a twig snap. Barely audible, she heard a charming voice.

"When the darkness opens wide,
Giving the sun a place to hide.
Dappled stars they prick the sky,
Blanket on which the moon will lie.
Why must daylight always dim,
Cower to dusk, so cold and grim?
'Tis the blackness of the night,
Teaches us how to see the light."

It was... a girl, in a greyish-pinkish shift up to her ankles, cupping a bluebird in her palm. Upon seeing Vesper, her gloomy expression shifted to one of felicitous. "Oh, thank goodness, finally, someone can help me!"

"Um, help? Uh, yes, I can help!" Vesper was confused at this change of pace, most of the *things* that had come out of the purple fog didn't have faces. Or voices. They dripped like tar, and when defeated dried up like paint and faded. Her face was too imperfect, too *human* to be fake."What's your name?" Vesper hesitated approaching, trying to negate the nagging feeling.

"Nerissa." She shook her dark hair. "And I don't need help, but this little fella..."

"I'm sorry," Vesper shook her head, finally relinquishing her hold on the dagger. "But I'm not a healer."

"You don't need to do anything," she screeched quickly. "I just need someone to guide me," she desperately grinned, like she didn't know how. "Please?"

Vesper caved. She hated seeing anyone desperate. "Okay."

"So, you're Vesper Dawn?"

"Yes." She raised an eyebrow at Nerissa cooing over the bluebird. She was... interesting. She talked very formally, like a grandmother. But her voice. "You're a very good singer," she remarked, "must have had a good teacher."

"Just natural," she replied breezily, "but I'm not from Nettle Town."

"Huh?"

She suddenly looked nervous. "Far too industrial for me. Would eat up little birdies like us." She shook the bluebird in her palm.

"So you've heard about the disappearances, then?" Vesper squinted, was the purple mist spreading? Nerissa didn't answer. "How much further?" Vesper probed.

"Just a bit further I think," Nerissa took a sudden turn to the left, into the thick mist.

"Nerissa, wait!"

So if she isn't a missing kid, then who is she? Vesper tailed after her. Then her thoughts stuttered to a halt. "But how is this..."

"We're here."

A gentle breeze drifted lazily through the clearing, the crystal air that hurt to breathe in. Grass strands were glowing, neon strands brushing the clear lake. Everything was just, "Too bright," Vesper muttered, squinting around.

"Thank you so much for leading me," Nerissa whispered in her ear, "you were very brave."

Vesper was too flustered to think.

"But you led me."

Adriana Curtis (13)

Penrice Academy, St Austell

The Cemetery

A slumping shadow appeared from the smoke that lay all around the cemetery. Shambling slowly. His eyes, bloodshot-red, fought to stay open. His nose was lumpy and portly and his eyebrows were thick and stretched. Doubled over, he was more crooked than his front two wonky teeth that were guarded by his chapped thin lips. He walked over to one of the graves with flowers in his hands. As his churned-up back, slid to the side, his wrinkled, scarred hand clenched into a tiny ball, threatening passers-by with his miserable smile. His scabbed finger lifted to a dented point as the wind swept through his ears, pushing him side to side, as his ghost-like face grew red with rage; he let out a scream of depression and sorrow. His threatening, miserable cry shot through the hearts of the village, making the children wake. His long grey dungarees hung onto his shoulders with dust gathering onto the surface of the buttons that used to be gold, but now were black and mouldy. Underneath his dungarees lay a black shirt and grey outskirts. There were rips everywhere, revealing bruises and scars. He sat by one of the graves. He lay down the flowers with tears filling up his eyes and some cascading down his cheeks. He said... "I miss you my love."

Rhiannon Hicks (14)

Penrice Academy, St Austell

Tea Leaves

On the top of a grassy hill, where sunflowers thrive, is my grandparents' house. They call it 'Sunflower Cottage'. Our house is the only one for miles, but I like it that way. Just Grandma, Grandpa and I. My parents aren't here though, they are in the graveyard, lying still with the roots. I never met them, but I am told stories about them. Grandpa loves telling stories. Especially ones about the tiny door at the foot of the stairs.

Hinges.

Rusty hinges.

I hear them every night. The only rusty hinges are the ones on the door, the door of Grandpa's stories.

Heavy rain and high winds are rattling the windowpanes and hammering on the thatched roof. I sit restlessly on my bed, my thoughts wandering through years of curiosity, through the depths of the stories of what lies beyond. Of what lies beyond the door.

"Tonight," I whisper into the darkness, "I will go."

Outside, the moon is shining brightly - brighter than usual - as I make my way down the hallway. I tread lightly down the stairs so as not to wake my grandparents. I reach the bottom and crouch outside the door. Afraid that I'll break it, I twist the minute doorknob with my fingernails.

The door opens.

Inside, there is an-

An-

An-

Empty room.

At least I thought it was empty, in fact, there was a minuscule red basket. It was smaller than a thumbnail, containing... Crushed tea leaves?

I hear a noise.

It's my grandpa asking for his evening tea. I carry the basket with me into the kitchen and place it by the sink. After boiling the kettle, I realise that the jar of tea leaves is empty. I decide to use the ones in the basket and take the steaming tea upstairs. The tea is a strange colour, probably herbal which is even better than normal tea.

As I drift off to sleep, I hear Grandpa's usual coughing (he has really bad asthma) and then silence. I think nothing of it and fall into the grasp of dreamland.

"Ben. Ben? *Ben!*"

I hear Grandma yelling and run into her room in only my nightie. Grandpa's name is Ben. It is worse than I could ever imagine.

Grandpa.

Is.

Dead.

The funeral is attended by many old people, family friends and my great-uncle Arthur. Crying and sniffing noises fill the church as people pay their last respects to Benjamin Charleston, a 'fierce friend' and 'caring brother'. My heart is torn as the cremation ceremony takes place, the kind eyes and loving arms of the greatest root to my tree of life is turned to ashes and placed into an ornate gold urn. At home, Grandma and I cry until our eyes run dry, clutching each other knowing that we'll never be the same again.

A few weeks later, Grandma asks me to do a special job and get the rat poison (arsenic) from in the little room. "It's in a tiny red basket," she says.

A.

Tiny.

Red.

Basket.

Izzy Hare (12)
Penrice Academy, St Austell

When I Become...

When I become a vet,
I'm going to help every animal I meet,
and own my own practice.

When I become an author,
I'm going to write a ton of books,
and attend book signings.

When I become a pro surfer,
I'm going to ride 100-foot waves,
and enter the biggest competitions.

When I become a doctor,
I'm going to invent new medicines,
and save loads of people.

When I become an actor,
I'm going to walk the red carpet,
and be on TV.

When I become a famous sports star,
I'm going to join my favourite team,
and win all the awards.

But, when I become older,
Who knows what I'll become?

Delphie Grant (13)
Penrice Academy, St Austell

No Man's Land (Rap)

Yo, I think that I'm stuck in no man's land, lemme abbreviate that for you
I ain't a so-called popular kid, but I ain't one of the school weirdos

Most rappers talk about differences but to you lot I'm just the same,
I'm just a normal teenager, no popularity or fame.

Those rappers I'm talking 'bout they say takin' shots to the head,
But mine just go top bins, bend like Beckham put it to bed.

Some people say rapping's easy that you get a sentence and make it rhyme,
But it's not that simple, trust me, 'cause I've been tryin'

When I said that I'm stuck in no man's land I mean that I'm stuck in the middle,
Tryin' to work out my future like man it feels like a riddle

Lately I've been tryin' to go viral, but I've been stuck in a downwards spiral,
All these singers on their socials, gettin' famous for their vocals

But I've just been rappin' rhymes, throwing it back to the old times,
Back when socials didn't matter you know,
Back then it was just me and my flow.

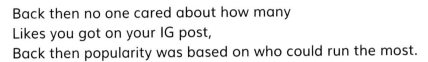

Back then no one cared about how many
Likes you got on your IG post,
Back then popularity was based on who could run the most.

Back then life was so simple, and easy,
But now you only get popular if you got the latest yeezies,

But that was the past, it was a blast,
But now in shops you gotta wear a mask,

Mask on the face, hide your identity and race,
Hide what makes us different hide your dreams and your
ambition,

Too many people trying to live life how it's so-called meant
to be,
But who's to say certain things should be a guarantee?

When you live in a modern-day society where everything is
acceptable,
When there's no rules or regulations you've gotta accept
people will be sceptical.

I mean, thinking people are gunna abide by the guidelines
Boris, let's get real,
Tomato pasta and a drink that's a Tesco meal deal.

The government trying to get people to stay at home and all
that,
But surely they know that half the UK are gonna ignore that.

'Cause you can't go trying to tell 70 mil people the don'ts and dos,
When half of them don't care about Covid 'cause they've got nothing to lose.

But that's not the problem in the opinion of mine,
I don't think it would make a difference if Boris were to resign.

Personally I think that the whole world is stuck in no man's land,
This whole Covid thing has definitely got out of hand.

So, I think that I'm stuck in no man's land,
I hope I've abbreviated that for you.

Daniel Rebers (13)
Penrice Academy, St Austell

The Earth Never Stops Spinning

The sun never stops shining,
The clouds never stop forming,
The Earth never stops spinning,
So we should never stop caring.

The trees never stop growing,
The flowers never stop blooming,
The Earth never stops spinning,
So we should never stop sharing.

The river never stops flowing,
The wind never stops blowing,
The Earth never stops spinning,
So we should never stop beaming.

Time never stops passing,
Fruit never stops feeding,
The Earth never stops spinning,
So we should never stop dreaming

The stars never stop twinkling,
The moon never stops orbiting,
The Earth never stops spinning,
So we should never stop trying.

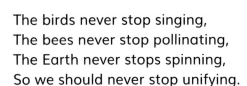

The birds never stop singing,
The bees never stop pollinating,
The Earth never stops spinning,
So we should never stop unifying.

Lightning will eventually stop striking,
The rain will eventually stop flooding,
Wildfires will eventually stop spreading,
If we stop harming!

Morveren Crouch (12)
Penrice Academy, St Austell

Lost

The sun gleamed with glistening joy through the pearl-like glass fixed onto the window. Joyous chants of birds could be heard outside. The floor was a caramel-brown wooden texture with a cloud-like rug with countless colours splattered across it. Everything was like heaven.

A miniature toy train could be heard parading around the room, followed by the carefree chuckles of a child scurrying around the room like a delighted puppy dancing through an emerald-green flower field. A woman could be seen relaxing in a beige rocking chair decorated with bustling flowers. The more the child's face lit up with joy, the prouder her smile grew.

The heartbreak of a window could do nothing but blare out to whoever was nearby. Many lost fragments of safety were splattered everywhere. Screaming, shouting and shrieking filled the streets.

The moon shyly peered through the sorrowful window as dust dragged around the ruins. A shattering roof shuddered above, trying not to uncover the moon's sharp gaze as the howls of the wind took over all sound.

A woman could be seen fixed onto a battered, dull rocking chair decorated with discoloured flowers and dust. Her body was rocking like a woodpecker desperate for more wood to peck at. Her icy breath stroked the charcoal remains of a sorrowful bear, almost begging for safety. Crimson-red stains were dried onto her battered, frozen face that looked as if it hadn't met the burning gaze of the sun for decades. She would be fortunate to disintegrate into dust by the blaring laser of the sun.

But that felt far from possible. Her world only felt like an endless abyss of obsidian, charcoal emptiness. Everything was like endlessly waiting, pondering in purgatory. Everything was dull.

Zoe Jackson
Penrice Academy, St Austell

Racism Speech

Hello.

I am going to talk to you about racism. I believe that racism is a huge issue in our society and that it needs to be stopped now!

Discrimination, persecution, antagonism.

For thousands of years, people have been verbally and also physically abused because of the colour of their skin. For example, in 1948 people were evicted from their homes and had to have pass books to travel anywhere outside their hometown.

Why have I chosen this topic you ask? I've chosen this topic because human beings are frightened to step outside into the world because they know that someone will comment on their appearance. Some people are ashamed of their own skin when they shouldn't be.

Nelson Mandela was sent to prison for 27 years because he tried to stop racism. Martin Luther King delivered a speech called 'I Have a Dream' to try and stop racism. For many generations, people have tried to stop racism. Now it's our turn.

Imagine, you wake up to go to school or work, you're in a good mood today and you feel like you can conquer the world. You go to school or work and all you can hear is, "Ew look at the colour of their skin." "Don't go near them they could hurt you or give you a disease." You would feel so embarrassed and ashamed of who you are. Imagine how that would affect someone if it happened on a daily basis, getting worse and worse. They could suffer with bad mental health and maybe even consider committing suicide.

So how can we help reduce racism?

There are many ways we could help stop racism, such as:

- Protesting to create laws to prevent persecution.

- Creating groups where people can discuss racism and think of more ways to stop racism.

- Teaching children about racism and why it's wrong.

You can do anything to try to stop racism, even if it's the smallest thing. The smallest thing can go a long way.

So in conclusion, I think that together as a society we can end the discrimination, persecution and antagonism against people of different races. Otherwise, in a few generations' time, there will be more suicides of innocent people who feel unwanted and think that they can't go on. All I want for this world is peace and equality. I think that eventually we can achieve that.

Baylee Morgan (14)

Penrice Academy, St Austell

Alone

Walking through the endless night
Looking for what is right.
People making me alone
I don't know where to go.
But the time will come when I find a home.
For looking back is not the key and
You will see the friends you have all the time.
Even though sometimes you want to cry.
Walking through the endless hall you find blinding light
Which guides you to the end.
People talking behind my back make me want to shout 'stop that'!
But I just smiled and walked away.
At home I want to tell but I just say I'm fine.
I am screaming in my head, but nobody can hear me out.
I feel like I need help but there's nobody I can trust.
I keep getting it wrong and people blame me.
Sometimes I feel like the weight of the world is on my shoulder.
I heard somebody cry out, "That's enough!"
I look up and see a hand. I reach up and have been saved
But when I feel down my good friend will help me out.

Zining Zhu (15)
Ranelagh School, Bracknell

Lost In The Clouds

Rain threatened London as ominous clouds bore over the city. In the streets, people skurried to cover like rats. All except one. He pulled his trench coat over his head as the first of many drops fell to the ground. The figure rushed across the cobbled road, heading towards a corner shop. Looking around to see if anyone was watching, he pushed open the creaking door as thunder boomed above him. "Bane! Welcome back."

The man, Bane, turned around to see an old woman. Her wispy white hair was combed from her wrinkled face, partially covered by a silken scarf, only bright azure eyes betrayed the lively character of the ancient librarian. Accepting a mug of spiced coffee, Bane walked to her desk, a wonderous clutter of notepads and broken pencils. As they walked, he noticed more people in the library than before, running their hands along the neatly packed bookshelves. Unlike an ordinary library, these books were turned away from readers, hiding secrets within the many pages. Taking a cushioned chair, Bane sat with the librarian. "There are more than last time, Alessandra," he muttered softly, turning a silver spoon.

"Yes, isn't it wonderful," the old lady exclaimed, "George, from last week, even brought some of his friends with him." She clapped her hands together merrily, causing a couple to turn their heads. Bane leant in, black hair covering his bespectacled green eyes.

"Miss Gizem, don't you think people will report Prism Library? There are some books that have become too dangerous to read."

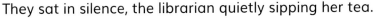

They sat in silence, the librarian quietly sipping her tea.

"You've come to return your book, I presume?"

"Yes, the citizens of Z'rbin are in safe hands."

"And you want another?"

Bane nodded, gulping down the rest of the coffee. He quickly stood, thanking Alessandra for the drink. Slowly, he gazed upon the seemingly endless corridors of paper, occasionally dodging the few people he encountered. Raising his callused hand, Bane caressed the books, searching for an adventure that called out to him. Suddenly, Bane heard a faint whisper.

"Help...me..."

He turned swiftly to see a book upon the floor, glowing with power. The closer he got to the pulsating pages, the louder the voice. Silvery-white streaks were leaking from the cursed book as Bane shuffled towards it, unaware of Alessandra's shouting. Swiftly, the book engulfed Bane and snapped shut, a copper lock clasping closed.

After a while, Bane awoke with mud streaked across his fine clothes. He quickly got up and hid by a nearby rock. Strangely, Bane's raven hair seemed to float slightly. His heart faltered when he realised he was upon a forested floating island. Bane looked over his shoulder, retching at how high he was: birds flew below him like ants upon a pavement, a thick layer of clouds veiling the possible ground that lay beyond. Collecting himself, Bane looked around him. A large house hung from the island, a lever system hauling great boxes. Bane realised that the building was powered on airstream power, lighting the building as starlit night fell. He stumbled towards it, opening the door, a splinter grazing his hands.

Inside, Bane was surprised to see a familiar room. Layers of books were upon the walls, their spine faced towards him. Oaken tables and leather seating were cleverly scattered across the room, a giant globe sat in the centre. Walking closer to get a better look at the world that he had entered, Bane could see that the globe was layered to show what was above and below the cloudline. Islands of all sizes and shapes were spread like jigsaw pieces above a darkened, polluted base. However, something was missing, making Bane's chest wrench in pain.

"Taken an interest in my globe, I see."

Bane's heart leapt from his chest as a pair of enlarged vibrant blue eyes stared back at him. The woman had a speckled face, luscious flaming red hair tied back. She tilted her head and giggled, her rough leather jacket exposing a strong feminine body. A corvid swooped down and cackled in the librarian's ear.

"He's the awaited one, Alexandra!" he cawed.

Alex examined Bane, making him shift on the spot. She pulled him up a flight of stairs to a larger table.

"If you truly are from the other side," she whispered, pulling curtains tight over shutters, "what is the librarian's name?"

"Alessandra, why? How do you know about my side?"

Alex puffed up, throwing her hands into the air, the bird flapping his wings in dismay.

"There's a page missing from this story, and I can't locate it here. I've been appointed Protector over the realm and of the portal and I can't abandon my post."

Bane couldn't believe his eyes as Alex took out a decrepit stone-engraved book, an obvious section of it missing.

"A portal? Is it possible for me to go back?" he asked.

"But you need to help my realm!" she shouted.

Bane didn't want to hurt Alex; she seemed to have been through a lot.

"If I can go back," he suggested, "I can find out if the page has been taken into my world."

Alex thought for a moment, nodding. She soberly took him to a separated wing of the library, a silvery-white portal whirring with arcane power. Bane took a last look at Alex, who was wiping away frustrated tears, before twisting back to reality.

He woke upon the carpeted floor of Prism Library.

"Are you okay, my dear?" asked a comforting voice. Alessandra.

Bane sat up, wincing at the bruising on his neck.

"Alessandra, where is that book?"

"What?"

"That damned book! Where is it, Miss Gizem? The one that I warped into?"

Alessandra rushed about like a hen, finally gathering up the book. It was strapped closed with a belt.

"What now, Bane?" Alessandra wept.

He looked at her, excitement in his voice.

"I believe that I have another voyage, Miss Gizem."

Caitlyn Street (16)

Ranelagh School, Bracknell

My Vampire Life

Dear Diary,

My name is Carys. I'm a vampire and I'm 13 years old. Wow, okay, that was blunt, but I am one. My cousin Ailill is also one, he was the one who bit me. The rest of my family are also vampires. Mom, Dad, my sister, and all my cousins and grandparents are too. I don't how they became one, but I know my story. I'll explain it.

When I was young, about 5 years old, I met my cousin Ailill. He had the same brown hair as me, and the same chocolate brown eyes. His skin was very pale. He was 4 years older than me, so he was 9.

I'd met him the day before school. I'd just started primary school, I was in Reception, he was in Year 4. I was terrified. Ailill walked me to school, and he was gripping my hand tightly. When we got to the school, he showed me to my new classroom. I stepped in and I could have sworn that all eyes were on me. I was jittery, I couldn't keep still, my ADHD was kicking in. My new classmates had already gone off in groups, and I felt like I was an outsider.

I saw someone coming towards me, a girl with blond hair, pulled into a loose plait. She looked at me and tilted her head and said, "So what's your name?"

I was surprised, I hadn't expected it. I stuttered, "O-oh, um my name i-is Carys."

The girl smiled. "That's a pretty name, Carys is. My name is Rosalind, but you can call me Rose." I grinned. I already had a friend!

When our teacher came in, she said that we could choose where we sat. Rose chose to sit next to me. I chose to sit next to her. We smiled at each other. If only I could tell how much this meant to me. Then I heard a cough next to me. "Ummmm, aren't you going to say hi to me? I mean, I am rich!" I looked to my left and saw a black-haired girl. She looked indignantly at me.

"Sorry, nope," I smiled tentatively at her.

At this, she erupted. "How dare you? No one says that to me! My mum is rich, don't you know? She can sack your parents from whatever job they have!" she shouted at the top of her voice, which was actually pretty loud.

People were starting to look. Oh god, I hated people looking at me. "Yeah, you try and do that! My parents are famous, you know that, right? Your parents can't sack them!"

Rose was looking at me with wide eyes, her lips slightly parted. "Oh yeah? What's their job, eh? Probably famous for being rubbish collectors!" That got a few laughs. She actually had no idea.

"No! They're famous singers." I felt like I was going to be sick now.

The girl looked at me properly now. "No, no, you're not..."

I sighed and held back a laugh. "Yes," I grinned. "I'm Carys Benzeguay."

Confused faces. "Emelé and Dêuce Benzeguay?" I felt everyone's eyes on me now.

"No way, no way!" screamed Rose. "No way! They are literally my favourite singers! Oh my god! I can't believe it!" This was all coming from 5-year-olds as well.

The black-haired girl sneered. "Well, everyone should know my name! I'm Isabella Spider." I laughed. "What?" she asked. I'm now roaring with laughter. "WHAT?" she yelled. I forced out between breaths, "Isabella... SPIDER! Oh my god! That is so, so, soooooo classic!" Then she lunged at me. She yanked my hair. I pushed her off and she punched my face, drawing blood.

Then Ailill was there, his face ravenous. "Um, Miss? I'm going to take Carys home. We got a call, and the office asked me to collect her." He dragged me out of the classroom, and out of the school. Then he looked at me and said, "Please forgive me for this." Then he bit my neck. I screamed. The pain was excruciating. I felt myself pass out in his arms.

Sky Priddle (13)

Ranelagh School, Bracknell

Fallen Angel

I was enthralled in ecstasy.
Tightly wrapped in the throes of nirvana.
I was entrancing, ethereal, enticing.
I was.
Now I lie, decaying.
Fading away.

Trees are gone.
Body burning, temperature rising.
Situation escalating.
Cold leaks into the bones of mankind,
Ripping, corrupting.
Freezing as the flames engulf me.
Suffering in silence.

Bella Chihota (15)
Repton School, Repton

James And The Giant Peach

James was a lonely boy
He had nothing to enjoy
He lived with two nasty aunts
So he wandered outside to the plants

James got given something magic
He fell over and dropped them, tragic
A peach began to grow
He thought it was going to blow

James found a tunnel in the peach
It was amazing what he came to reach
He meets creatures including a centipede
Then the peach began to roll at high speed

James and the creatures became friends along the way
With many challenges they survive okay
They make it to New York across the sea
Finally they are all free

Then as quickly as the peach had grown
A huge parade was thrown!
Everyone danced and cheered
With no more nasty aunts to be feared.

Christopher Squibb (13)
Southview School, Witham

Stronger

I have been learning about bones and muscles
And to help us get stronger, we should eat good food like Brussels
Our body has around 200 bones
They feel as hard as stones

Our bones and muscles help us to move
And with exercise our muscles can improve
The bones protect our organs like our heart
So looking after them is really smart

Muscles control our heartbeat
And help us run like an athlete
So it's important to keep your body good
Just like we all should.

Lewis Sargeant (12)
Southview School, Witham

Zoo Diary

Dear Diary

I went with Dad and my mum and Holly to the zoo.
On the way to the zoo, I felt excited.
At the zoo I saw fish and tigers.
My favourite part of the day was seeing the seals.
I could hear all of the birds.
It was very busy, there were a lot of people.
I was very happy because I had a good day.

Love from Charlotte.

Charlotte Freegard (9)
Southview School, Witham

Faerie Rings

I wish I could step into faerie rings
But instead of my name they'd take other things

Like my red rosy cheeks and distorted proportions
My annoying-sounding voice and my mind's own contortions
My dead-looking eyes and my strange-looking hair
And the way I zone out with a cold vacant stare
And the way that I act when I'm with those I know
The way that I cry when real life starts to show
And the fact that I feel every motion on my skin
Which makes me want to collapse and rip them out from
within

I wish I could go to the shops and order
All the pieces I want like a selfish little hoarder
And attain all the features some assembly required
And create a new person that's actually desired
Who knows how to shut up and be kind and act right
Who doesn't feel the need to write two stanzas about how
he feels at night
And who doesn't feel the need to be everything he's not
And everything he isn't in a stupid made-up plot

I wish I could step into faerie rings
And be someone different afterwards.

John McGowan (14)
St Andrew's RC Secondary School, Glasgow

111

Blood, Poems And Christmas Dinner

The cold doorknob welcomed my hand as I pulled the door open, a blade of light tore through the curtain and onto the piano keys, the gold stripes of light lay on his right side, complementing his features. Dragging him through hell was all that crossed my mind. Sparks on his fingers from trying to keep a hold on, eyes like shattered battleships sinking to the bottom of the ocean and like the warm sand that hauled him deep beneath, filling up his lungs just like contemptuous and intolerance filled him now. His lips were the colour of the purest blood which folded at the sides like a curve of a heart. The snowflakes melted on the glass behind him but some stuck to the ground forming a thin layer of white snow.

"There are ten people running around the kitchen preparing dinner and you're playing the piano?" I asked.

"More like five people, we don't have ten people living here," Ambrose argued.

"I didn't know I had to be that specific with someone who can't do basic maths, add one onto that number and come help in the kitchen," I demanded and left.

I walked back through the cold corridor. The hanging paintings were filled with ire and darkness to the last brush of paint, and the warm light from the chandeliers held up the ceiling.

I walked into the kitchen which was soaked through with the smell of turkey and burning berries. Adam screamed to mix the berries that were far from edible now, the whole room was filled with warmth, cinnamon, and a hint of stress.

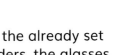

Freeing myself of the tension, I went to see the already set table; the red candles snuggled in their holders, the glasses at each plate admiring the table, plates holding each other and wearing the napkins as ties.

As everyone gathered around the table the flames on the tall candles danced crazily, cracking jokes and folding in laughter. Panic was building in my chest, and piece by piece the panic started to travel through my body, forming a knot in my stomach.

The people gathered were fitted in their most elegant outfits, many with pearls wrapped around their necks and enough hairspray in to use a bottle of shampoo to get it out later. They looked around with noses and chins pointing up, and with eyes filled with envy. When everyone did their round of loathsome looks the forks and knives started battling for the food gathered.

Once everyone was finished and the clock announced that it was 8 o'clock, the crackers were passed around. The people who hadn't left to admire the snow outside had already wrapped their fingers around their crackers and we started to count down.

Ten. Smiles spread across everyone's face. Nine. The smiles reached their eyes. Eight. Their eyes grew more curious. Seven. The dancing flames reflected in their eyes. Six. A knee bounced up. Five. The liquids in glasses splashed around. Four. The forks danced on the plates. Three. Fingers tightening their grip. Two. Eyes shot across the room as a cake was carried in. One. The eyes drilled into the crackers and with a few snaps laughter filled the room and small glass bottles, candles, crowns and pieces of paper fell out.

As the cake arrived at the table a few slices of oranges slipped off and found themselves lying comfortably on the plate. The room lit up in laughter again before everyone settled for a slice of cake whilst looking at the small gifts that snapped out of the crackers before.

A few had their paper crowns on and smiles painted across their faces as they read the notes, this year we decided to put a note in for someone else and seal up the crackers. Ambrose, who sat opposite me, stopped everyone to read out his note, he held it up and showcased the Christmas border around it, it was a poem. With crumbs falling from his lip, and a quick inhale and exhale he started reading:

> My pens will write letters with your blood
> the devil will love you dangerously,
> as your parents cry at your grave
> stiffness in their body, fullness in my heart.
>
> Grace will leave your grave
> when the shadows come around
> stillness will stay within your muscles,
> just like the heartache within others.
>
> The stars splattered across the night sky
> will look down and wish upon your grave
> as you're dragged down,
> nails marking themselves on the coffin
> as your hands slide down.

As the last line of the poem slipped from his tongue the grin on his face disappeared and was replaced with a worried look, cheeks puffed and eyes red, holding back tears.

His lips changed into a darker shade of red, and his mouth dropped open. Tongue red, bleeding, and his chest dropped rapidly before rising again repeatedly.

People scrambled out of their chairs that curled themselves into the wooden floor and retreated far from the table. His lungs attempted to grab more oxygen, finally he took a sharp intake of air before choking out blood which covered the table between us. A few more coughs and people ran out the room, leaving us alone. The blood-soaked table matched the red flowers and his head fell into the plate, smashing it.

I wiped the splattered blood off my face with a napkin. I pushed the chair back and the sound of my heels filled the room. I pushed his head back and checked for a pulse that I knew was absent. I put my phone torch on and opened his eye, the pupil seemed to dominate the brown in his eye. Turning off the torch I looked for my father's number. When he answered I broke the silence. "He's dead," I said clearly.

"Are you sure?" the voice on the other side asked.

I looked back at Ambrose, his head seemed to be tilted back further and answered, "Yes." The line was silent again.

Wiktoria Krosny (16)
St Andrew's RC Secondary School, Glasgow

New City Champions

One day a new virtual reality game called New City came out and was a big hit in the gaming industry. It was basically a game where people could buy new avatars, vehicles and skill points for quests which could make you the New City champion, who was currently trapped in the game. It was such a big hit that after a few months an evil talented hacker hacked the game and anyone who logged on could not log back out. That means he had basically kidnapped almost half of the world. It was such a scandalous scheme that New City was banned.

Three teenagers took it upon themselves to try and take back the game. So they implanted an anti-virus into three headsets which could mean they could get in and out. They knew the risks but decided to go as they were the world's only hope, as no one was as skilled as them at the game. They entered New City and saw it was as cheerful as an old lady's party. Everyone must be so sad as they couldn't get out the game. They had to go and find a weak spot in the game to implant the code that Josh made or, as he liked to be known when in the game, Thunder.

The weakest area in New City was the Sky Castle. It was so big the hacker hadn't fully taken over. They had already looked for the weak zone to implant the anti-virus before they entered. The Sky Castle was far away from the spawning point, therefore they used their vehicles to get there.

Zoe, known as Sabre, used her rollerskates which she named Flash, while on the other hand Aaron, or his gamer tag name Flare, used his hoverboard called Firebird. Like a hungry wolf Thunder jumped into his car with confidence. They were going to save the city.

Thunder told them they only had thirty minutes until they had to log out or else they would be stuck there forever. Shocked at how much time they had left they sped down the street like an angry cheetah. Once they reached the Sky Castle, some robots who looked like babies had just lost their dummies.

Thunder said, "He must have put some kind of defensive coding to stop us." They knew that to save these innocent people they had to fight.

"Thunder, get to the top, you can use Firebird but whatever you do don't lose that blade," said Flare with great urgency. (The blade was the anti-virus.) Flare and Sabre summoned their weapons.

Like an F1 car, Thunder rushed to the top of the building but more security soon caught up to him. Unfortunately, he knew he couldn't outrun them so he had to fight.

Suddenly, he started to regret coming in without more backup. Somehow he took out his weapon and realised he forgot to upgrade it, as it was a level 7 weapon which he knew couldn't do. He didn't have any credits left. By the skin of his teeth he realised Firebird had lasers.

But back down, Flare and Sabre were getting outnumbered big time, then that's when out of nowhere the New City champion Eagle showed up and helped them win the fight. The Eagle was highly respected by gamers.

Thunder had also won his fight, he was hurrying to the top. Sabre's Flash could fly and the Eagle had a jetpack to fly up. Unexpectedly, Flare was the only one who couldn't get up there. The Eagle saw he was stranded, then gifted him a jetpack. Confidently they all flew to the top gracefully.

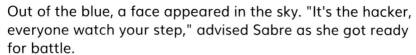

Out of the blue, a face appeared in the sky. "It's the hacker, everyone watch your step," advised Sabre as she got ready for battle.

"I will not let you ruin this for me!" shouted the hacker. Then crazily a dragon flew down with a sense of authority. "Let's see how you deal with this," cackled the hacker hysterically. Thunder needed to upgrade his weapon, therefore he asked Eagle for some credits but instead he lent him a level 83 sword, then said, "We are going to need all the help we can get."

They ran into battle like they had no life. They battled and battled but the dragon was just too strong. Then Flare remembered he had a very rare item card from one of his quests before, that could combine any four weapons into an ultra weapon. They all retreated to find shelter. They laid four of their best weapons on the floor, then Flare put the card on top of the weapons. Then the unexplainable happened, all their weapons turned into one giant super weapon which surely should be enough to destroy the dragon.

The weapon needed three people to hold it, therefore one of them could get the dragon's attention. As Sabre got the dragon's attention the rest of them lined up a shot. Their aim was spot on as it took the dragon out.

Then they ran up to the top and as Flare was about inject the game with the anti-virus, he was abruptly interrupted by the hacker again. This time instead of shouting he begged them not to do it but why shouldn't they? Therefore Flare stabbed the blade into the top of the castle and now everything turned back to normal. People were logging out and logging in. They felt a rush of joy and relief.

Eagle was so impressed after they told them what they did that he gave them a gold badge which means they were heroes.

Once they logged out, on the news was: "People are suddenly being able to log out of New City."

Unsurprisingly they felt a sense of success and achievement. They were happy with people knowing who they are in the game and not in the outside world. They were legends forever no doubt.

Legends never die.

Daniel Taiwo (12)

St Andrew's RC Secondary School, Glasgow

My Box Of Secrets And I Am The Key

Such dangerous claims and powerful affirmation, in this world where only I exist, where the ruler is no one but me. In this small, narcissistic world where I am no one less than the protagonist, its only disadvantage and advantage being no one but me.

Entangled between a mere dream and a full new reality, where nothing is possibly exposed from here, my box of secrets and I am the key.

In my imagination, I am taking a bath by the beach, the sea is as pink as cherry blossoms in spring. Up above me, I can comfortably watch the sky, whose clouds are raining teas, their colours vary from east to west but as you watch the whole view it's a paradise and a fascinating sight to see. However, as much as humans may want power to keep, I only want a body to live.

I don't call my dreams a dream, if so I am as lucid as I can be, I have lived for years in this Neverland where Peter Pan doesn't dare to visit.

In reality, perhaps I am like Aurora taking her eternal sleep, regardless of whether I have a prince or not, it's almost impossible to wake me up from this sleep. I am not dead! Not yet.

In the morning, when I am no longer the queen, nurses and doctors pass by me, they are treating me as docile and sweet. I would like to claim that I am awake, but their voices pass by me and my eyes don't move, my body doesn't obey me, it's as if my time stopped while the whole world kept on moving.

I thought of sleeping by, watching as the years decay my spotless baby face to one with thorns on. I watch as they explain to the kids, it's only puberty, as they worry for their bodies' changes.

But not me!

"I no longer have a dream!" I say, furiously accepting this hard reality that I take back and sleep.

Trapped in this hospital bed, which I wholeheartedly want to escape, the scent of sedatives and blood always wandering around the rooms and corridors, making me nauseous, such intense scent! I think.

That's the reality I don't want to accept to be in. I am praying every day, give me a life or take me from it.

"It's boring to pass by such repetitive days like this."

Once again, my world takes shape, it's as expected as I wanted it to be, I am diligently flying, taking a light stroll above the clouds which form a stair and a red carpet so that I could pass as a queen.

In my mind, pretty boring pink dresses of princesses are as disgusting as they can be. Somehow red and black colours seemed to resemble more my feelings of vengeance, hate and, as terrible as it can be, the jealousy is a large part of me.

Such useless feeling, says who? If our life wasn't full of comparisons of in-between, perhaps friends and family who take accomplishment as a natural competition and start to compete, wouldn't always compromise to such a baseless defeat.

Perhaps I wanted something different for the day to pass by as quickly as the thriller, which always passes on the hospital TV while the most important part of the movie was to be revealed.

When I am inside my lucid dream, I can still faintly hear reality as a sound of mosquitoes outside the window, I hardly pay attention because as interesting as the lives of other people may be, at night it's still a nightmare with the sounds of cries and screams of patients and family members.

Today was a little different, I could hear loud noises troubling me as I could recognise its hoarse voice clearly, turning myself off from my lucid dream. Unfortunately I hear a scene that I don't want to.

"Let me die, please?" Somewhere in my heart, I suddenly bless the fact that this scene I can't possibly see, but I can still hear. I hear the loud and louder screams that the woman beside me gives. Her story makes it harder to ignore, poor her! I think.

As rich as she is, spent twenty years of life in a coma and once she wakes up from her sleep, she can't understand that life didn't wait for her. Her husband, who she loved so much is now married to someone else, her best friend died and she lost her job. In her mind life isn't worthy living any longer.

I want to comfort her, no one understands her like me. The doctors pass by and watch her tears, she pleads with them for death and they still don't want to hear.

I have always kept track of how much I can control of this strange event such as the lucid dream.

Mostly my knowledge from the outside world is from the exploration I do in the common people's minds. On that path I have seen too many dreams and personalities, their daily lives are crazily complicated.

Some people would scare me and other annoy me, if a normal person saw as many minds as I did, there is no way they would keep their sanity intact.

Moving on its own, my virtual body slowly opens the door of hell, where I can hear the thoughts and emotions of someone else and that makes me feel miserable. I don't want to go to such an extent, if they had heard her earlier I wouldn't have done this.

It's hard and complex, the human brain, and in that inescapable labyrinth I have found a path where I can take people from this earthquake of a life and I do.

It leaves no traces and doesn't hurt at all. That's my secret locked up in my box of secrets, and I am the key.

Nelkelly Rodrigues (14)

St Andrew's RC Secondary School, Glasgow

Under The Moonlit Night

Raven drummed her fingers on the windowsill, her left hand cupped under her chin. The moonlight bathed the room in a silky silver. She looked out through the window with a distant far gaze. She could only stare as far as her eyesight would allow, it was as far as she could go. For the city was in the dark, not a soul lingered in the streets.

The home, a supposed refuge, had become a cage blocking them from contact with the outdoors. She was much too young to know how it had started, she was less than one. But despite her young age she knew that this was not how things ought to be.

Yuan stretched out her legs, leapt up onto the armchair, and curled herself into her owner's lap with a soft purr as she settled to fall asleep. Benjamin's old hand stroked her gently as the cat breathed ever so slightly in its sleep. Benjamin had aged to the point that he was awaiting his time. Then, he had wanted his time to come long ago. Then he wouldn't have to experience such dreadful things. Life was cruel to him. Now an old man, what more was left to do?

If only he could turn back the clock, when tulips still bloomed in all vibrant colour. When he still had a glint of hope in his eyes. He struggled to remember how things once were. All was in a mist of unbearable silence. Constantly being watched closely. Every move so much as a twitch was being recorded. He wondered what caused a human to create such a restricting system that only brought depravity instead of life. How far will someone go to strive to become God? It would take all of time and whatever out of it to just swipe the surface. What a fool to cause such sadness for something so selfish.

Benjamin wanted to stop thinking about such and he closed his knowing eyes falling into a deep sleep, drifting away in his dreams.

Wilhelmina was packed and ready. Her house was due to explode and she, for one, didn't plan on getting caught up in that. She was a gun. A gun that had been on lock and load too long and was about to set loose. A dog held in captivity for a lifetime and had finally remembered how to bare its teeth.

Unlike everybody else, she wasn't going to be caged. She wasn't going to be a zoo attraction. She wasn't going to stay in the dark for any longer.

She crept down the hallway with her metal bat grasped tightly in her hands. You could hear the quiet creaking of her footsteps and *crash!* One camera came crashing down, then another, then another.

She barged through the door and darted across the lawn to the car on the right. She whipped out her keys, clicked open the car and started the engine. The car roared to life, like the dust had been lifted off. She cranked it up to top speed and sped off. She knew she didn't have much time. They would be coming for her soon.

She could hear the sirens ringing from afar. She could see the faces peeping out their windows to see such an act being executed. They gathered to witness the beginning of a new era. Everything was on the line. She kept peeking in the side mirror as she drove on the road that led directly out of town. She knew they would be awaiting her at the borders. She already knew how slick and sly these guys were. She swerved and took a different route. Who said cars needed to remain on roads?

She could see them now, pelting behind her. Flashes of red light shot at her as she spun round the wheel, trying to steer clear of the deadly beams. She took the ray gun from her bag, tipped herself out the window and sprayed red beams nonstop. She kept glancing forward to check where she was exactly driving to. One of them was coming from overhead. Their beady eyes scanning around from afar. Embers flickered in Wilhelmina's eyes. She had come prepared. The gun changed shape and moulded with her arm as one unit. She propped it up and sent a massive ray of light right up into the sky and instantly the clouds were split and a metal body shot down. Its cogs and screws spilling everywhere. She knew there was still more to come, she needed to make haste. She had already mapped out where the border's blind spot was and as long as she found a way to divert their attention, the chances of escaping would be more than slim. The car slugged through the dark woods. Her mind was in a whirl. A glint of silver came from her left. She ducked straight away. Both windows suddenly smashed immediately, shards of glass flying everywhere. Some cut away at her skin but she didn't falter. She shook shards out of her afro.

She had gone in too deep and there was no looking back. She stuck her arm out and began to fire. There were more snipers awaiting her. Drones poised. More of them on her tail. She warded them off one by one as the car clumsily spun through the woods.

The border was in sight. She turned left and started down diagonally towards the border. She saw the metal box that she had researched for years.

The box that holds all the border together. She gathered as much firepower in her arm as possible and let loose. She didn't stop to wait. She drove right through the border in its fit of smoke and flames.

Wilhelmina sighed a sigh of relief. Years of hard work had paid off. She drove down the road - the first soul it had had in a decade - being closely watched by the moon that glowed beautifully in her wake.

Oluwakayode Oluwole (13)

St Andrew's RC Secondary School, Glasgow

The Unknown People

Useless. Unhelpful. Wicked. The words constantly repeated in my mind as my eyes opened with shock. Was I dreaming? Surely not I hoped.

It had been almost a day since I hurt him and the words were already sinking into my head. *Have I damaged him that bad?* I asked myself before the words surprisingly repeated again. It was honestly giving me a headache but I couldn't stop it. Could I?

It was almost like I was imagining things. The walls were getting closer. The roof was shaking. My head was spinning. I screamed, "Help me! Help me!" But by the time I said that I was already knocked out.

I opened my eyes sharply and questioned the room. It was pitch black. No noises were heard. Was I hallucinating? The only thing I wanted to do was get out of here, but suddenly there was noise.

The confusion caught up to me. What was happening? As I was thinking about how I would get out of this dark hellhole, the noise made its appearance again. I wondered what it was, but in the distance I saw a dark thing sitting. I thought to myself, *is it a trap, what if a monster grabs me?* I said, "Nah! Monsters ain't real!"

I finally built up the confidence to slowly take a few steps over, but stopped in my tracks as I thought to myself again. *Is it safe, will I be safe?* The likelihood of me being safe was very high so I didn't suspect a thing.

I continued to walk slowly. The ground had a reflection of me. When I was a step closer to the black thing in the corner, it started to say a very weird message. It repeated, "I'm sorry but you will never escape this hell hole!" It said it over and over again.

At the same time, the words in my head began to constantly repeat themselves again and again until it made my head sore. I passed out in a matter of seconds.

I woke up as fast as lightning and tried to scream but couldn't, something was holding my mouth down, it wasn't a good feeling. When I tried to move my hands, it felt like I was chained down. The chains felt like the Titanic holding me down.

I heard a slight noise coming from the bottom. I thought I was the only one here. My brain finally came to its senses and thought, *is there a real-life person inside this horrifying place or am I just hearing stuff?* I decided to look around the room to see what weird stuff lay here, but then I realised I was chained up to a chair so I couldn't move.

I scanned the room with my eyes, it seemed like a demonic satanic room since it had a very devilish and diabolic spear circling the room. It was almost like I was in Lucifer's demon hole, which made my blood curdle and sent my spine chilling with fear.

There was a problem though, the steps were getting louder and louder by the hour, maybe they were taking their time? Who knows, but this place was making my fear for people much worse.

I saw a tool in the corner but couldn't identify what it was, but if I tried to move I might fall down. My trust in humanity was fading away... I felt like there was no escape. This was the end of it all. The words pierced in my brain, "Useless. Unhelpful. Wicked. Useless. Unhelpful. Wicked. Useless. Unhelpful. Wicked." Would it ever stop?

I was trying to scream but my voice was all muffled up by this stinky thing on my mouth. I heard someone come up the last step... was my faith in humanity restored? Who had come to save me from this demonic place? I saw a dark figure, but the strange thing about it was that it had red coming from the back of it, which confused me a lot.
I closed my eyes and then looked again, but this time it had moved closer to me. Almost like it was doing juju or witchcraft. Hold up though, only Satan had powers like that... "Wait!" This couldn't be happening. It was the real-life demon slayer! My muffled screams couldn't contain my excitement.
I think I was mistaken though for something else... As it walked closer to me, I moved back my chair. As I moved it again I fell down. I was screwed for sure. My blood ran cold with fear. I had never felt so petrified in my life before... My heart was racing faster than a cheetah could run.
I realised it was a satanic figure but I couldn't see the face, it was almost like its face had been ripped off by something. As it came towards my face, its long fingernails punctured my eyes, blood shot out as his other hands perforated into my brain.
I couldn't feel a thing. My blood-curdling muffled scream left me shocked, but as he went deeper my veins started to pop out as blood exploded everywhere. His head turned into teeth that bit my soul whole, tearing my whole body apart. My last vision of the world was him swinging my head with enjoyment and munching it all down in a second and him laughing viciously, like he didn't have a care in the world. No wonder he was demonic.

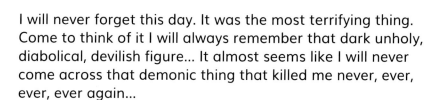

I will never forget this day. It was the most terrifying thing. Come to think of it I will always remember that dark unholy, diabolical, devilish figure... It almost seems like I will never come across that demonic thing that killed me never, ever, ever, ever again...

Fatmata Diallo (12)

St Andrew's RC Secondary School, Glasgow

An Unforgettable Experience

This world was a world that was full of life, hope and loyalty. But later the world turned into a mess due to everything that was going on.

On a warm and bright morning the sun shone brightly in the sky. There was a village girl whose name was Emma. Emma lived a happy life with her mother, who goes by the name of Julia, and her friends. Emma was a teenager who had a beautiful body shape.

When her mother died she was so depressed. In her village there was this disease going around called smallpox. Her mother got this disease and also a lot of people. Her mother died of this disease and she had to live her life by herself. She described the world as a dangerous, harsh and strict place. Emma had to work to be able to gather money for her to be able to buy food and other things she needed. After gathering a little amount of money, she left the village and went to the city.

On getting to the city she did not have a place to stay, she was living on the street until one day she met a girl named Alex. Alex was a drug addict, she helped Emma and took her to her home. Emma started living with her and one of her friends whose name was Frank. Frank was an assassin (who are the people hired to do some dirty jobs or even killing other people).

Because Emma had started to follow these people she started doing notorious things and she became one of the notorious girls in the city. She started drinking and she became a drug addict.

132

Emma was a very lovely and beautiful lady but because of the fact that she was so addicted to drugs she looked so ugly.

After about two months of taking drugs continuously, she started having some brain difficulties and damage. Emma left the house due to her brain damage and started living on the street again.

After a year of living on the street one of the boys named Ben, who knew her and fancied her back in the village, took her to a standard hospital and she got treatments for almost three months. The doctor advised that she stayed in the hospital for examination and later when she left the hospital she started living a new and better life.

Emma went to the university. Since she had gone through secondary school and had an outstanding result she was able to get into the university.

Emma had always dreamt of being a medical doctor but because of all the challenges she had passed through she killed her dream, but now she had the opportunity to accomplish her dream.

A few years later she had accomplished her dream. After that she went back to her village with Ben. Since Emma had become a medical doctor now she helped the sick people in her village. She also helped little children and made sure all of them were educated and also accomplished their dreams. Emma and Ben had become very close friends after he saved her, Emma didn't like him at first but later she gradually opened up her heart to him and after a few months they had started dating and they already fixed a date for their wedding.

After their wedding, Emma and Ben became a great couple and they always helped children. They went to the orphanage and helped sick children every time.

After Emma became a doctor she frequently travelled around the world to do some severe operations. Emma became a very popular surgeon, she had been called by different high-standard hospitals to come and perform some surgeries.

Ben on the other side was a CEO. He was the CEO of LK Goods and Services Industry. Ben was a well-built young man, he was well matured and the prayer of all women. Ben was a very cold person, he didn't smile at all in the office. Ben didn't like women being around him apart from his wife.

A few weeks after their wedding, Ben and Emma went on their honeymoon, they chose to go on a vacation on the sea or ocean for at least a month.

A few weeks after they came back Emma started having signs and symptoms of pregnancy and she later confirmed that she was pregnant. After nine months of pregnancy she gave birth to a girl who she and Ben named Anna (which means grace or favour) Mercy.

Emma specifically chose this name for her because she believed she'd found favour in the sight of the Lord and Mercy because despite all she had passed through, God still had mercy on her.

A week after the baby was born she got sick and died. Emma was in deep sorrow and she cried all day. Two weeks after the baby's death Emma got sick, she got sick because she just gave birth to a baby through caesarean section (CS). She had not been resting because of the sudden death of the baby, and because of this the wound she had during the operation had not healed and had also been infected.

Due to this Emma died two days after, which was a bad experience for Ben. The two most important people in his life were gone. But he was sure they were in a beautiful place called Heaven which made him happy, and he was sure that one day he would finally reunite with them when the time came.

Esther Akinola-David (14)

St Andrew's RC Secondary School, Glasgow

Welcome To Hawkins

Some people think that Hawkins is cursed. I mean, they're not way off, they just don't know the whole story. I've been living here for a while now, but nothing's really been that bad before. Like sure I get the panic when some kid goes missing for like a week, or malls catching 'fire' and a bunch of people die.

But I was always able to handle that, I was never in town anyways when anything interesting happened. At least I used to be. Now there are kids from my school being murdered and the whole town is in shambles. I want to just pretend that everything is being blown out of proportion as normal, but I don't know how much longer I can do that. Maybe I'm not getting the big deal about this because of how used to death I am.

"Oi, adventurer," I hear a voice say as I'm lost in my thoughts.

"Yeah," I say quietly as me and my friends are hanging out in the local scrapyard. I'm currently sitting on the roof of an old bus.

"So, what are we going to do?" Sammy asks as he's playing with a pocket knife.

"About what?" I question.

"About the murders," Sammy replies.

"I don't see how that applies to us," I say as I smash a car window with a rock.

"Amy, we all know these killings aren't normal," I hear Henry chime in.

"Yea, none of us would be worried if it wasn't for the way those bodies were left," Alison says.

"Not to mention, we did break into the morgue. Those bodies weren't killed normally," Tom explains.

"I guess... you're right," I stutter as I don't want to admit that something's going on but... "Can someone hand me my crossbow?" I ask as I lie down on the bus roof.

"Sure," I hear Susie say as I'm given my brown crossbow with some metal arrows.

It honestly feels like the world is ending and I'll be dragged into the chaos somehow. I always am. I point my crossbow up at the sky before producing a flame of fire from my hand and I light up the tip of the metal arrow.

"You guys don't think Joey and Nathan are involved, right?" I hear Susie ask. I shoot the arrow from the crossbow up in the air before wiping the ink from my nose.

"No, this is different. It doesn't seem like their work. But it feels familiar," I answer.

"How come?" Henry asks.

"I... I don't know, it's just a feeling," I stutter as I lie on my side, and look at the inside of my right arm to see something that's haunted me for the longest time. My black number tattoo. 023. It's just familiar.

Amy Millican (15)

St Andrew's RC Secondary School, Glasgow

137

The Dance Of Death

A blurring swirling black abyss,
the tenderness of her shadow's kiss.
Perplexingly plucked from all I know,
and taken to where we all will go.

I writhed and I tried to escape her embrace,
until she graciously unveiled her face.
Her spectral skin as white as fresh snow,
her eyes glared as a shard of ice glows.
With one focused look and no words uttered,
I knew what must happen; my mind uncluttered.

I march and I glance at those that I join,
for the dance of death shows both sides of the coin.
A king, a beggar, a mother, a butcher,
together we unite under an uncertain future.

Every man here has a death that awaits,
but they once had aspirations, loves and hates.
They had a mother who loved with all she could express,
and a lover who yearns for one last caress.

We tread and we march on into the distance,
still attempting to accept our own non-existence.
We refuse to realise there is no horizon,
no neatly made graves for our bodies to lie in.

138

We can search all we want but -
there is no light,
there is no light.

Sophie Greig (14)
St Andrew's RC Secondary School, Glasgow

Gone

Gone, disappeared.
No one heard the name Kayleigh for a long while.
No one knew where she went,
No one particularly cared.
Memories she had with friends,
Were never ever shared.

The frustration and anticipation,
The jealousy and betrayal.
Her friendships fell apart,
It seemed they had turned stale.

The tears would flow,
All wet and slow.
Her face was pale and sodden,
Her fun memories at the time, were briefly forgotten.

They clearly weren't aware,
They made her miserable.
They treated her so badly,
Completely inconsiderable.

She'll be fine though,
She learnt a lesson.
Don't be friends,
With those who give you depression.

Gone, disappeared,
But not forever.
She will find better friends,
Some that are better.

Kayleigh Cassie (14)

St Andrew's RC Secondary School, Glasgow

Peace Is All I Need

Kindness is free,
Rudeness is a choice.
If you want violence in the world,
I will certainly disagree.
You have to stand up for yourself,
You have a voice.
There were many people who stood up for rights.
They wanted their voices heard.
We can follow in their footsteps,
If we spread our wings and fly like birds.

Alexandreau Djoh (12)
St Andrew's RC Secondary School, Glasgow

Jasper's Disappearance

Chapter 1

Autumn breeze. Tyler was sitting under the blossom tree watching the sun set as the pink wispy petals were falling softly on him and the ground but then...

"Hey Tyler have you heard from Jasper?" Hope shouted while running to Tyler.

Tyler sat, confused. "No I haven't spoken to Jasper since yesterday at the tree house why?" Tyler said, confused

"Jasper has disappeared, he isn't answering mine or Stacey's texts or calls!"

exclaimed Hope.

"He'll be okay, have you looked at his favourite spot?" Tyler said.

"Stacey already looked at the tree house he wasn't there either," said Hope worried.

Tyler thought to himself it was strange, Jasper always told his friends where he was going something was up.

"Let's go home before it gets dark."

They both ran back to the village just as it turned dark and eerie.

Eva Fotheringham (12)

Stirling High School, Stirling

Crashing Down

I suddenly awoke from my interesting dream which was something about travelling in space. It doesn't really matter to me. oh well I guess, It was at the back of my head. I'd had an idea, while I was struggling to remember, my mum sharply called me to get down immediately! I stumbled down, grabbed a piece of toast and rushed to school. I was dozing off in maths. "Emery, answer this question please?" "Uhh t-d... h, sorry." I had forgotten to do my homework! "See me after class please."

Oh no...

Later at lunch, I was talking to my lovely friends and something they said while talking about science reminded me of my idea. I had wanted to build a rocket ship and go to the beautiful moon! I immediately started hurrying home. At this point, I didn't at all care about school.

"Emery where are you going? Come back!" my friends called.

The second I got home I scampered to my mini workshop and began crafting. It took almost seven whole hours just to begin the insulation. I had to go to bed so I briskly got ready for bed, I closed my tired eyes and swiftly fell asleep.

"Three... two..."

The noise of people counting down gradually got louder and louder.

"One!"

I opened my eyes in shock to the feeling of moving upwards, my surroundings were patchy bits of scrappy-ish metal and glass windows. The moment I looked out one of the windows, I saw the whole city from the height of drones, watching it get higher and higher, it was now at aeroplane height.

It got even higher to above the clouds! In fear, I burst out into tears but at the same time, I was so excited as I'd always dreamed of space, as the tears rolled down my face and slipped to the floor like rain I had sudden confusion. How did I get here?

I started panicking with thoughts like, *did I get kidnapped? Is this a test?* I was clueless as to what had just happened. Suddenly the spacecraft started shaking. I looked out the window and noticed I could see the moon gradually getting closer and closer and closer! It was so near I could barely see its surroundings. As a rush of fear went to my brain I sat back down and tried calming myself, I noticed that there was a spacesuit so I decided to put it all on, except for the helmet to save oxygen. I was about to arrive on the moon and as I was landing I came to an immediate conclusion, I should use the buttons' panel to try to contact a space station! As I tried to figure out each button's use I felt the spacecraft shake but I didn't know what it was and then... I saw it, a *big* red button.

Breathing heavily I pressed the big button...

"Hello this is the space station speaking, how can I help you?"

"Uh... Hi, I'm stuck on the moon and I need to get back to Earth. Can you help?"

"... I'm sorry I can't help with that bye."

The person talking had hung up and not helped! I was mind blown, it was as though my heart had dropped the height of a skyscraper! I panicked and pressed another button. I sat in silence for a while. It was so silent that you'd be able to hear my own heart beating. I kept waiting but I still couldn't hear or see anything happen. I was still waiting after a few minutes but still nothing happened.

I decided to try to comfort myself by lying down on the bench, after a little while I fell into a deep sleep. After I woke up I realised out of thirst that it was almost day two of no water and that if I didn't get back in time then I'd die tomorrow! My throat was as dry as the Sahara desert which made me feel I could barely move, stiff as a board. I reached for the button panel to look at it and see if I could figure something out. I dragged my finger across the panel, across all the multicoloured buttons. "Green is my favourite colour so I guess I'll press green..." Slow as a sloth I pressed the emerald-green button.

Beep, beep, beep, beep! An alarm started, I felt the ship shake and the alarm went off, then the small bulky ship was moving but not towards Earth... it was heading in a straight line toward an asteroid! It looked as though if I hit any part some would head to Earth, it was a massive asteroid. I was scared as a child and innocent as a lamb. As the asteroid was getting closer quickly I thought about my family and decided I'd press another button, at the speed of light I pressed the yellow button... It only half worked but I went from getting closer quickly like a cheetah to moving slowly like a snail. Weirdly the ship started going in zigzags and up and down and then it stopped completely, I was so happy that I wouldn't crash but then it started moving again but this time it went up and towards the asteroid again but it went so close I saw my life flash before my eyes. I opened my eyes to see half of the asteroid heading straight for Earth. I screamed in pain as I saw it was going for my country.

Meanwhile, all the electricity stopped working except for one button. It was glowing violet. *Such a beautiful colour*, I thought to myself as I reached for it. I took a deep breath as deep as the grand canyon, and then I pressed it. A rush of adrenaline hit me as I hurried onto my seat and watched as the earth broke to pieces. Then I woke up from my dream. "Emery come down for breakfast!"

Isla Forrest (12)
Stirling High School, Stirling

For I Have Sinned

It's dark. Like a TV showing films in black and white. Like someone putting a pillow over your face. Eyes open or closed, it didn't make a difference. I stifled back sobs as they were carried past me, wishing it could be different. If only it was me and not them. Bouquets of dying, wilted flowers decorated the seats, all the wrong greenery for a funeral. There were no tears. Simply hoards of people putting on masks, playing a game, acting in a film, pretending to be affected. None of them really knew what pain felt like.

Dozens of people putting on sad faces as the bodies were lowered into the ground.

My eyes opened, no longer willingly suffocating in the world of sleep. Voluntarily trapped in my duvet cocoon, I willed my eyes to stay open, desperate for the time to pass slower. Desperate for everything to come to a halt, so I may enjoy these few blissful moments with less trepidation of what will come after. The trepidation of leaving my sanctuary. The fear of facing my sins.

I exhaled slowly, scanning the barren walls as I gazed at the solitary cross on the wall. The pleasing combination of dust and grime in the bedroom kept it suitably heavy. Weighing down on those who dared to enter, ensuring that burden, that guilt, that consciousness was ten times worse, making sure you were aware of your crimes. It was a prison. The cell had little to no personal effects, except for one printed-out photo, an altar to the dead. The bed used to be comfortable, all of those heavenly pillows and blankets that made you feel like you were lying on clouds. Now it is a wooden frame, the springs knives, stabbing you in the back every time you lie down.

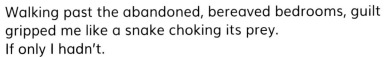

Walking past the abandoned, bereaved bedrooms, guilt gripped me like a snake choking its prey.

If only I hadn't.

I wearily drifted into the colourless kitchen, preparing myself for the wave of disgust that would consume me. Keeping the sick down, my body burned with hunger. In front of me lay a desirable-looking platter; a cornucopia of fresh delicacies like perfectly cooked bread drenched in golden butter and see-through jars filled to the brim with bloody scarlet jam. I couldn't allow myself to enjoy such luxuries, to feel such pleasure.

Not after what I had done.

Not that she understood that.

There she was. Describing someone in one word, hers would be 'simple'.

She was a simple woman.

She had a simple personality.

She had a simple mind.

And she had a simple understanding of me.

Wearing a constant look of dismay I could feel her beady eyes judging all that came into the proximity of her tunnel vision. Her snake-like tongue was only visible to those who could see past their own large, empty head. I could feel my own vocabulary slip in her presence. I wasn't her daughter.

Her daughter would have faith.

Her daughter could be saved.

"Heron, food."

"Heron, food."

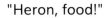

"Heron, food!"

The words shattered out of her mouth, flying out in fragmented pieces like glass, straight into my face, carried across the air by a now destroyed salad-covered plate.

She hurt me.

Like I hurt them.

I subtly grabbed a knife off the table before I swivelled round, intimidatingly pushing my face right up in hers, snarling as we locked eyes. The cross she wore around her neck swinging gently, veins see-through and clear, anger burning in both our eyes. As we continued to stand off, the TV blared about some unimportant, boring news broadcast. I snatched an apple off the table, holding it up to her face as she started to back away.

She could never understand it, never get it, never know the truth.

I closed my eyes, exhaling loudly as the tip of my finger dug into the knife's edge, blood streaming down my hand as my mind flashed back. Back to where it all started. Back to where there was blood everywhere. Back to where the car was covered in it. If only it was mine, and not theirs. As I stormed out of the house, I knew my penance was not enough. It does not make up for what I did. Only one thing can make up for what I did.

Only one sin.

I was going to meet the fire and the brimstone, the purgatory that lies beneath our feet. I was going to meet the Devil. I was going to go to Hell. I needed to make sure I went to Hell. I needed to make sure I'd get the punishment I deserved.

I needed to make sure I burned.

One foot glided in front of another, a smooth symphony of moving forwards, my mind buzzing with productivity as the clogs finally started to turn. Clasping the knife, I could feel its smooth metal handle, its surface without flaws. How I envied it. Gripping the knife tighter, I knew what I had to do. Guilt. It is something we all experience, something we all feel, something we all despise. It is something we all have to live with. Something that creeps in the darkest depths of our minds, something that slithers and crawls, something made of pure evil. It is something hated, our desperation for a clean slate overwhelming, a guilty conscience frowned upon. And how do you find the punishment you deserve? How do you deal with the guilt? Do you repent and pray for your soul? Or do you swallow fire and burn down the church with you in it?

Heather Cook (15)
Stirling High School, Stirling

The Deep

3... 2... 1

I began plummeting into the water, the fall rattling my bones. My heart pounded in my chest as water surrounded my vision. Everywhere I looked there was water. Very few fish swam in these cold waters, hopefully I wouldn't find any bigger ones today.

"Let the submersible sink before you start moving," came a voice over the intercom.

"Roger that," I replied.

Above me, dark gun-metal grey covered the sky. Thunder shook the vehicle and lightning hid in the clouds. I could see a yellow arm of a crane above me through the ocean, the same crane that dropped me into the sea. After a minute of waiting I could hardly see the bottom of the boat through the murky, dark water. My briefing was quick and confusing but I kept to the plan, after all, if everything went how it should I would have enough money to buy a house.

"Please proceed with care," came the voice again.

The submarine lurched forward as the engine started. A dull hum came continuously from behind me and every few moments I could hear a high-pitched beep coming from one of the many instruments. I sank deeper until I had reached the correct depth.

"Depth: 3,000 feet," I stated proudly.

Silence.

"I have reached the specified depth," I remarked, a hint of impatience in my voice.

A shiver ran down my spine and a sinking feeling began in my chest. I examined the area around me, I was nearing the end of the twilight zone, a midway point between the blue of the ocean's surface and the complete darkness of the deep sea. In front of me I had a multitude of buttons and levers. Everything glowed a dim red. I switched my headlights off. Nothing. All I could see were small species of plankton floating past idly, just like small particles of dust. Suddenly a frightening sound came from the radio. In-between static I could hear panicked voices. To my dismay, I couldn't make out very much.

"Does anybody copy?" I spoke, trying not to let my fear show.

In a matter of seconds, I was upside down. My head smashed against the glass in front of me and water spilled in. I was completely disoriented, I couldn't tell if I was the right way up or upside down. My eyes flickered and soon I was surrounded with water, the pressure almost crushing my skull and making it impossible to breathe. The excruciating pain was made worse when I realised the water around me was red with my blood. A row of teeth sank into my leg and as I began to lose consciousness I heard the radio.

"Do you copy? Do you copy?"

Everything went black.

Ewan White (15)

Stirling High School, Stirling

The Snow Warrior And Sun Hope

In the heart of Yokohama, Japan, where the rich are pampered and the poor scavenge, where the tallest tower in the world blocks out the poor and the rich with the rich living at the top and the poor living at the bottom, the new bodyguard knocks at the smooth, wooden door. He wields a long bow almost half his height with a pack of arrows.
A beautiful Japanese mansion that sits on one of the highest levels of the tower with the view of the clouds, blocking the sea of vagabonds and slums below. He is one of the unlucky few born unfortunate. Sakura blossoms gently fall from the trees, as he waits for the door to slowly open to show a man with neat clothing and posture. Unlike Yuki wearing a kimono with stitches on it from being torn multiple times.
The man glares at Yuki up and down. "We don't give change..." he says.
Yuki sighs in annoyance. "I'm the new bodyguard, Bushida Yuki."
The man at the door chuckles at his words. "Impossible, you don't even have armour!"
Yuki is annoyed at his assumptions. "I can't afford armour."
The man is sceptical until the head of the house appears. "Come on now, this is the vagabond guard I was talking about."
Yuki bows forward as he is finally welcomed in where Samurais with well-made, shiny metal armour look down at the young archer. The head of the house Mr Kiko starts a small talk with him. "I'd love to thank you for accepting this job."

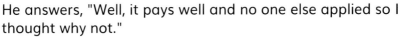

He answers, "Well, it pays well and no one else applied so I thought why not."

Mr Kiko then tells him what he primarily needs to do. "My daughter, she just reached her age of 18, she's blind and being from a rich family she's an easy target for kidnapping and ransom. I just don't want her to grow up in a box forever, I want her to find someone she could love, of course not you."

Yuki nods his head in agreement with Mr Kiko's demands.

They reach her room, it is a huge metal door that is almost impenetrable to anything. "Her name is Hinata, please keep her safe."

Yuki bows his head and the door opens, multiple cameras examine the door for anything that could be dangerous.

As he enters the door closes and cameras gaze at him at every corner, he sees a girl sitting on a chair humming and playing with her fingers.

"Kiko-sama, I am at your service!" He bows to her but she turns her head.

"Are you another bodyguard?" she asks, her voice humble and sweet.

"Yes."

"I never get an archer as a bodyguard, by your accent, you're not from these levels, are you from the lower ones?"

He is shocked by her assumptions as he stands up. "You can tell that?"

She nods her head. "I normally hear the vibrations of things to know what a person is holding, you wield a bow and you are currently carrying 63 arrows."

His expression is shocked, the two begin to bond.

"Kiko-sama-"

"No, call me Hinata, I don't mind."

Yuki is shocked by her words, he's never got so personal with a higher-level person before.

"I want to get to know you since you're gonna be protecting me."

Her smile is almost as warm as the sun and Yuki feels his chest have a small pound. But he ignores it.

"What is your schedule?" he asks.

"Normally I head out into the garden with a bunch of Samurai and I head back inside, that's my day."

He looks almost shocked. *Is that it?* he thinks.

After a few minutes, he leaves her room. "You shall begin tomorrow."

He is given a single room, it looks a bit dusty with old stuff that seems to have been lying around there for years with broken shelves. "Surely you slept in much worse, enjoy." Mr Kiko leaves the room, leaving Yuki to himself. He prepares himself to sleep. He tosses and turns, thinking about his home, as he begins to sleep in the bed peacefully.

By dawn, he is up training the other Samurai who mock him and two of them decide that they want some fun. They are taller and bigger than him. "You, come and spar, we promise to not do too much," says one of them.

Yuki walks up to them and as they take their stance, the two attack him at once, giving him a disadvantage but, in a second, both of them are on the ground.

They both glare at Yuki who just walks away. "You need to improve your skills, especially in judo."

Yuki heads into the garden, gazing at the cherry blossoms and the sea of clouds.

A few minutes later, Hinata appears by his side. "What is it like?"

He is caught off guard by her arrival. "Um, lovely, so much that I don't think I have the right to even look at them."

Hinata turns her head to him. "Why?"

He answers with his head to the ground. "Because of my status."

"To me, that is a silly reason, we're human, nothing more, nothing less, we both bleed red and have the same organs."

Yuki looks to Hinata with his heart almost feeling light and comforted. "I know it's weird to ask but can I feel your face? It's just that to me your face is a blur and I just want to know who my bodyguard is!" she requests.

He is unsure but allows her, sitting on his knees as she caresses Yuki's face.

"You have such lovely skin," she says to him in her angelic voice. "I bet you're quite popular down below!"

He chuckles. "Quite the opposite actually, mam, my parents weren't the best people so... yeah."

Her face is still pure as can be. "I hope I can get to know you, Yuki-Kun."

They go back inside ready for the next day...

Antonella Dionzon (15)

The Adeyfield Academy, Longlands

Metropolitan Hell

Five years ago, this place was just a field. Used by no one. Cared about by no one. It was a rare spot, uninhabited by humans in a dying world. 90% of the world was covered in cities, another 9% covered in landfills, this large field was part of that 1% that had almost no human presence. However, the world was overcrowded, governments needed to find new places to destroy for living space and with a world population of over 15 billion people. This was no easy task and many drones were sent out, when they found this field, in the middle of nowhere, untouched by humans for over 500 years.

Of course, it didn't take too long to turn this small natural jewel in an industrial hell of a wasteland into one of the biggest, most modern, most technologically advanced cities in the history of humankind.

An environmental hell, this city emitted more carbon dioxide than the country, not too hard when you have a city the size of Northern Ireland. Unfortunately, this 'environmental hell' happened to be my home.

I love the environment. However, seemingly I'm the only one in the entire world who feels this way, which has resulted in my life being a long, pathetic tale of failed dreams of restoring the Amazon Rainforest to living in the most environmentally unfriendly place in the world. So how did this happen to a person who dreamed of devoting his whole life to the environment? I hear you ask. Well, to put it simply, I was forced by the government as a sort of twisted punishment for me after I caused them so much trouble in Brazil and various other countries.

Anyway, I'm not really sure that anyone actually likes living here, apart from the rich and wealthy of course. Whilst the city is the most advanced in the world; you could order something and have it delivered within a few minutes or be called poor for not having a flying car, which are as cheap as chips. However, the higher powers, namely supreme leader Cardis, are extremely manipulative and controlling and monitor your every movement, unless you're rich enough to bribe them.

Anyway, every conversation is heard, freedom of speech is just a myth here and the slightest word against our supreme leader can get you executed in the most brutal ways. Of course, as technology has evolved, punishment has also evolved, just backwards. Just count on the human race to come up with more and more creative ways to injure and kill each other. I'm probably risking my life just by writing this: I'm starting a revolution. Whether I can find any like-minded people or not, I will storm the capitol building with the intention of Supreme Leader Cardis not escaping alive. I will probably be killed, or worse, be captured alive and tortured to death. But death is better than watching everything that I ever stood for slowly be crumbled to dust. However, when devising my plan (mentally, of course, anything written would be seen by the ultra HD security cameras implemented into every single house and apartment), I was approached by a problem instantly, doing this alone would be a suicide mission. That was my problem, any friends and family would be on the other side of the country and it wasn't like I could call them either due to traced phone calls.

Then I remembered, there was one person who worked with me out in Brazil where we had a lot of practice making plans behind the government's back. So much so that we made our own code. Surely it was worth a try. So I texted him in my code, which probably wasn't so secret, but I think he got it, judging from the winky face emoji he sent back. One part of the plan is done, now we have a two-man team to take on the entire government. Sure, if a government official happened to look at our messages, it might be a tad obvious, but that was the least of my worries for now.

It was dead on eight o'clock when I heard a knock at my house. That was the first strange thing, David was never on time, it was either early or late, never dead on. Regardless, I walked to the door and upon it pretty nonchalantly, anticipating greeting an old face, instead, I was greeted with a faceful of fist and instant unconsciousness, that was the second strange thing.

I woke up in a dingy dungeon, presumably underneath the complex that was the capitol building. My head was throbbing with pain and I was badly bruised all over my body.

I slowly got up, my neck aching like nothing I'd ever felt before and I was greeted by the face of supreme leader Cardis, smiling like a menace.

"Geoffrey Thrust," he said in his deep, booming voice. "I sentence you to death for treason against the state."

My stomach dropped: they saw our texts, I was done for. A sliding door ahead of me, made of heavy industrial metal, slowly opened and one of my hands was unshackled, one fist against a fully armoured gladiator.

Straight away he approached me and lunged at me with his spear, grazing my stomach. An agonising pain shot through my body, however, his spear had become lodged in the wood that I was shackled to and I saw an opportunity... I grabbed the knife from the gladiator's belt and stabbed it in his back and twisted the knife.

As he tumbled to the ground, I looked up at President Cardis and gave him one manic, but smug smile.

Oliver Hutchings (12)
The Adeyfield Academy, Longlands

Autism

All I can see in my mind is fear and stress. What is going to happen in the future? I ask. Will I pass my GCSEs? Will I get a job? Will I have a home? Will I reach my dream career? Autism is a spectrum, there are many different aspects to the condition. Everyone with autism is completely different. Autism is nothing to be ashamed about, I can't help having it. I was born with it?

"You are on the autistic spectrum, meaning you have autism Robert." Only just a few months ago, these words came out of a therapist/doctor's mouth after a long assessment and them two having a chat together, deciding if I was autistic. The words made me freeze, my heart sank. I later broke down into tears. It feels scary, it feels upsetting and at the moment of hearing these words, it makes me feel ashamed. Self-doubt, question, worry, sadness, consciousness, anxiety. This word looks like a constant crying child due to the many barriers people with autism face. It is not an excuse, it is something that needs support and people with autism need guidance, help and attention to allow them to feel happy. I feel like I have to act 'normal' at school and that I cannot be myself, I have to do something called masking and it is so hard to try and be 'normal' because if I don't act 'normal', then I will be picked on and potentially bullied.

Autism is just like any other condition like asthma, it can be treated and although autism cannot go away, it is not a bad thing on its own. Because people with autism have a larger brain and extra capacity suggesting that there is too much going on in the brain and so the brain gets overwhelmed very quickly. However, this can be a positive thing as it allows people with the condition to think quickly and have many ideas.

Autism is not a scary mighty monster, it is just a way of thinking and a different way of looking at life but people with autism are just like other people in many ways, they still have eyes, ears, a voice and everything else that is attached to the human body. All that is physically different is the brain being slightly different in an autistic person.
I know that I can still achieve what I want and that I will pursue my dreams and I will reach them because I am never going to let my autism stop me from doing what I would love to do in my future.
"Autism is not a disability... It is just a different ability" - Dhar Mann - American producer, creating YouTube mini films based on everyday morals.

Robert Vinyard (14)
The Adeyfield Academy, Longlands

The Real Recipe

Willard Wilbur Wonka Morley, known as Willy Wonka, was a truly unhinged man, he was way over his head in debts and payments. He could not afford to keep the factory open or at least to the standards of his prized customers.

One day Wonka had a rather ingenious idea, or so he thought, if the factory was the problem he would give its own swansong per se. What child would turn down the opportunity to go to one of the most famous sweet factories?

He planned one of the biggest events in the franchise: five gold glorious tickets spread far and wide across the globe. When Wonka launched these sensational pieces of paper any ticket found was a press sensation, the tickets were awarded to a variety of children: Augustus Gloop, Mike Teavee, Charlie Bucket, Veruca Salt and Violet Beauregarde. Wonka was pleased with these children and their liking towards different types of treats.

When the children were invited into his factory, they were slightly stunned by how unpleasant Wonka's meeting skills were but the unusual occurrence was that he already knew all their names but they let it slide, the dark truth was Wonka planned for these kids to get the tickets because he desperately needed a new plan to keep his possession up and running against all the strange wacky sweet stalls. Then the idea clicked, what could be something... new... something... tasty? It sounded crazy at first but Wonka was not a man with intuitions. He thought that maybe if he incorporated... organic scores into his candy it would taste more succulent and for sure would sell like crazy.

But Wonka needed to make sure that this plan would work. He elaborated a scheme for each child in some room that would definitely tempt them to give in to their candy cravings.

He thought that Augustus would make a delicious chocolate strawberry swirl or violet would become a mouth-watering tropical blast bubblegum sensation! Mike was used to finding how far the taffy could withhold stretch, Veruca was used to see what waste mechanisms worked but Charlie he was special, he was invited to show how very lucky he was to be raised with principles and rules. He was shown to not take your life for granted and he was lucky for that.

Wonka had soon found his new recipe...

Chloe-Leigh Sanderson (13)

The Adeyfield Academy, Longlands

If You Go Down To The Woods Today

Never did I think a walk in the woods would be as horrifying as this...

I ignored the gut feeling that I gained the second I stepped foot in the maze of trees and I foolishly journeyed ahead. The sharp ends of the branches that pushed out looked like they could kill in a blink of an eye. It was like the thick depths of the bloodless, ghost-coloured fog was trapped but given a specific order to suffocate all life.

The forbidden leaves that lifelessly fell to the floor breathed heavily. Suddenly, all darkness was saturated with a threatening, bulging light nosily staring down. The little confidence I had left in me vastly drained into the night.

I tried turning back, the trees had replaced my footsteps. There was only one way out. With the lack of positivity I had grown, and the doubt that replaced my hope, I was sure this was how it ended.

About an hour had passed and I wondered how I hadn't woken up from a dream yet. As the night grew, so did my goosebumps. I instantaneously dropped to the crisp leaves, lowering my hands into what looked like a curdling river. I leaned my weightless and near-empty bag against the moist log I rested on. I knew the only way to survive would be to set up camp until morning.

I dedicated my little energy into making a fire out of the flint and steel I had smartly remembered whilst packing for this so-called 'adventure'. Succeeding in fire-making gave me a little inspiration.

I positioned myself on the log in the warmth and safety of my little fire. It was a long and cold night, yet I blinked and within the flash of an eye, it was dawn.

Now it was light I could see how terrifying the forest truly was. Everything I had seen the night before was the biggest understatement of my life.

I knew I was in for it, I knew that this is where the nightmare had truly begun...

Jessica Hinks (12)

The Adeyfield Academy, Longlands

Fly

As a young girl, I wish to know what it felt like to fly. Here I am, fulfilling that wish. Standing, on top of the building, the wind rushes to me as if it is saying goodbye. Closing the proximity between myself and the edge the feeling of emptiness crawls through my veins, leaving tingles on my skin.

I step once again, as the city lights fill my eyes, making me smile before I bid my final goodbye. I step for the final time. I'm off the edge.

Freedom courses through me as my hair dances in the wind. *I'm flying*, I think to myself, even though I know that my wings will soon disappear from my grasp.

I am now a part of the wind, falling gracefully into my darkness. I am living the dream of hopeless little girls but, someday, these girls will know the real meaning behind flying. That flying is so peaceful and welcoming but yet it is so uncanny and sickening.

It finally hits me, the darkness that is within me takes over. I am now the darkness within the wind.

Taylor-Shattar Smith (12)

The Adeyfield Academy, Longlands

The Intergalactic Crisis

Years ago, there was a portal underground in the United States of America. Alarms blared with the red crosses. The PA shouted, "Defcon 2, all military personnel please be present at the gate room."

"What the heck is going on?" said a man in his bed. He was woken up by the sound of the portal. His name was William and he was a part of the SGOC (the Stargate Special Operations Command) tasked with exploring off-world planets such as Thenia and such.

"C'mon, let's head to the gate room, something exciting must be going on!"

They rushed and swiped their card at the gate room entrance there and they saw the portal shining with reptile-like creatures which looked like snakes but standing on two legs.

"Go on, SGOC units, go explore the Goa'uld Empire!" the commanding officer said to them.

"Did I hear that right? The Goa'uld Empire was an empire and successor of the Anubis Empire! Although they were weaker than the Anubis empire they were one of the strongest empires in the universe's history!" I thought aloud to myself. I chose to enter the Stargate, unaware of the dangers ahead. Then I remembered the other SGOC before me that entered the Stargate and showed up in the Goa'uld Empire that came back with less than half of their original numbers.

He entered, unaware of the ambush... "Whoa, is this the Goa'uld Empire?"

The empire was full of trees and sand. Suddenly the next set of SGOC came and a colossal explosion occurred behind the portal, killing the next set of soldiers in the SGOC force.

Then he saw the horror, all of the Serpent-like soldiers but not combined with Horus soldiers, that came out of nowhere and blasted the soldiers.

"I never expected the empire to look like this!" shouted William.

The troops tried fighting back but the bullets did nothing with their armour and they forgot to equip their suppressors!

They quickly put it on and were now able to kill the serpent guards until... A flash of lightning came down, killing some soldiers. There they saw the god Anubis, a supreme system lord of the Goa'uld Empire. He had a weapon of some sort that teleported them all to the Goa'uld homeworld of Gamma and the SGOC were then thrown back through the Stargate onto the Earth.

Sixteen billion light-years later, after the Stargate portal was destroyed the AFPU and the SGOC went on a mission of war against the Goa'uld Empire. The war and fighting was brutal and Anubis was killed by a weapon used by the SGOC, while the other SSL and SL all fought bravely throughout the entire war which lasted for over a thousand years.

At the beginning of the war, the legend William S Johnson killed six thousand Goa'uld imperial soldiers which was a great success but when returning to the base, he was shot.

Death toll: The total of deaths in the Intergalactic Civil war was around 77 billion deaths in the entire war.

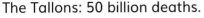

The Tallons: 50 billion deaths.

Planet Status: Destroyed

AFPU including others: 5 billion deaths.

The Goa'uld Empire: 20 billion deaths.

Empire Status: Fallen.

The Second Goa'uld alliance: (Classified.)

NID, SF, SRT deaths: 2 billion deaths.

Palyn Thongtan (10)
The American School Of Bangkok, Thailand

Fake Mask

There once lived a fawn. The fawn's name was Raiden. His neighbour was mean and bad. He lived alone. He even tried to commit suicide but the police were there to save him, so it didn't happen.

He met a person called Kamado Ichigo. Kamado Ichigo was very kind and sweet. They started to talk and play together. They became friends.

After one month went by, they became best friends. Raiden was very, very glad that he didn't commit suicide because if he did, he wouldn't have meet Kamado. He was still a little sad though because his neighbour was still making fun of him. "How rude!" Raiden complained.

However, one day, a random werewolf came to Raiden and said, "Oh, hi Raiden, you seem so sad. I have this magical potion from the magical island, if you drink it, you will be so powerful and strong that no one is going to bully you again!"

A random person requested him to drink it.

Kamado tried to warn Raiden it was a bad idea, but Raiden wouldn't listen to Kamado, so he drank the potion.

He fell asleep immediately and he woke up again in a scary, dark cave. Everything was dark, he couldn't even see oxygen.

"Hello?" Raiden shouted. "What have I done? It was the worst mistake," Raiden sobbed.

"Well, well, well, you shouldn't have drank the- ah-hhh aaad-dsfsssg gfdhsdjfvhsyf nhuesvgiuhu hsgiusbhufsenh abnonfaniuarhfdfdfdgsfgs dyfgshdvgdsfsfnfbvsgyfgvhs bghsdbgvdhvbdhgbdhfg bdffbd svbhsdbvfgdrbgfbvsg..."

"Hi, I know that right now you guys are very confused, well I hacked into this story and I'm going to upgrade it," Mysterio explained. Mysterio is now controlling the story. "Welcome to 'choose your ending'! You can all choose your own ending. There is a happy ending, mystery ending, time loop ending and magical ending..."

Happy Ending

"Anyone there?" Kamado shouted with confidence.
The werewolf went out to look and he saw Kamado.
"Found you little twinky pumpkin eater!" Kamado giggled.
"How dare you call me that?" the werewolf yelled! The werewolf jumped to Kamado with his full speed.
"Oops too late," Kamado chuckled. The werewolf was captured by the police outside and taken away.
Kamado and Raiden lived happily ever after.

Mystery Ending

After the werewolf captured Raiden and took him to a scary, dark cave, Raiden was never found again.

Time-Loop Ending

Raiden is trying to find the way out! He looked everywhere in the cave while the moon was watching, until... He found a small, shiny, beautiful, green rock under the food plate.
"Ooooohh, what is this green rock?" Raiden said to himself.
"It's called a timestone, you can use this timestone to travel in time, you can go forwards, you can go backwards, or you can even stop time," a random person answered him. He used the time stone to travel back three days.

"Oh, hi Raiden, you seem so sad. I have this magical potion from the magical island called Gruinard Island that if you drink it, you will be so powerful and strong that no one is going to bully you again!" a random person requested him to drink.

"No! I won't fall for your tricks anymore!" Raiden replied.

"Oh no, the trick won't work," the random werewolf said to himself, shaking in his mind.

If you talk to someone in the past, your life will become a loop. Raiden travelled back to the present and the werewolf put him into a dark room for two days. He punched the room a lot of times until a random person came in and helped him out but he was caught by the werewolf but Raiden had escaped already.

Ridden travelled forward two days. He went into a random cave located in Ohio while riding his scooter and so he went inside. "Aghh, this is so complicated because this place is very dark!" he complained with an exhale.

He heard a person punching a wall, he followed the sound and he saw a person in a room so he helped him out and then he got caught by the werewolf and was captured there...

From that time, his life became an infinite loop of punching walls and helping his past self. Did he get stuck in another universe?

Magical Ending

Raiden couldn't find any way out, but he read an ancient book called: 'The Book of the Invisible Sun'. This book had so many powerful magical abilities, he could remember only a few of them.

He could remember 'Astral projection', 'Parallel World', 'Energy blast', 'Protective Fields', and 'Divine Conduits'. All these powers are powerful. He practised some of them, which made a loud noise.

Raiden tried to calm himself, Raiden's brain needed to relax because his body wasn't doing so well. Raiden drifted off to sleep.

The next day, the werewolf came to take Raiden away while he was loading his memories back into his head and the werewolf pulled him very hard. All of Raiden's memories went back into his head and the werewolf punched and scratched him very angrily. *Skrrreeek!* The scratching sound was very loud.

Raiden was hurt and had to meditate to use his powers, the power he used first was Parallel World (another name for Parallel World is Multiverse).

"It could be that our universe is just one member of a much grander Multiverse, Multiverse suggests that our universe, with all its hundreds of billions of galaxies, almost countless stars, tens of billions of light years, may not be the only one!" He recited the curse with a full tongue.

Raiden used a parallel world to confuse the werewolf, then he used the finishing ability called 'Astral Projection'. Astral Projection is to push the enemy in the chest and your enemy's soul will jump out of their body.

Raiden used the power to stop the werewolf. As its soul left the body, then he put the werewolf's body in a secret lab. After about one month, people saw another werewolf that had lots of powerful abilities...

Nattatam Jam Suavansri (10)
The American School Of Bangkok, Thailand

The Mermaid Crystal

On a nice day at a beach, an acrobat was lying on her towel, enjoying the weather. Her name was Anabelle, Ana for short. "Another cup of that lemonade please!" she said to her trustworthy waiter.

"On it Ma'am," he said. The waiter ran to the bar and came back with a lot of lemonade.

Ana saw how tired he was so she said, "Go get yourself a drink and enjoy the beach!"

"Thank you so much, and remember you have a show tomorrow!" he said.

Ana smiled remembering. "I'm going for a walk now, enjoy the beach!" she yelled as she walked away.

She walked to the rocky waters and saw a shimmering waterfall! She couldn't believe it so she went closer to take a photo but the waterfall disappeared! Now it was just some shimmering rocks!

"I must be daydreaming," she said, slapping her head. As she walked away, she looked back. The waterfall was back! She then decided to take a selfie and posted it. It said: 'At a beautiful waterfall in Hawaii!'

Then everyone in the comments said: 'That's just a cave!' or 'You must be dreaming!'

Ana was confused, she walked closer and closer then discovered the cave the viewers were talking about. She walked towards it, luckily there was a small hole she could fit in.

She went inside and saw crystals, jewels and even Jasmine's heart! (A rare jewel that was for someone but fell off the ship when it was being conducted off). She then saw... water in the cave too!

She looked inside and saw beautiful corals shimmering in the cave. The fish were rainbow and she found a chest and opened it...

"A-a-a m-mermaid crystal!" she gasped. When she touched it, she felt like she was going to grow scales (because mermaid crystals turn you into mermaids).

She touched it whole and turned into a mermaid! She jumped into the water and looked at her beautiful scales. She thought, *I should keep this a secret for the mermaids!* She laughed and then she went to the surface and turned human! She was ready for her show until she heard a small 'eep!'

She looked back and saw a cute little merkitty! She picked it up and saw its little blue eyes like hers, the merkitty had the same scales as her and she had a collar that said: 'Rose'. *Rose*, she thought. Grinning, she took Rose but Rose stayed there whining. "Huh? What's that?" Ana asked looking at a note. It read: 'To Anabelle Stan, you are now the keeper of Rose, the cat. Her favourite food is tuna or cheese. She loves to sleep and stay away from lighthouses. From the foam spirit, Ariel'.

"The foam spirit? Ariel? What? Did Ariel turn into foam?" Ana asked Rose.

"Yes it's true..." came a soft eerie voice coming from below... Ana remembered the voice immediately! "A-Ariel?" she stammered. "Where are you?"

She looked all over as she spoke. "Down here, Ana."

Ana looked down and saw a foam shaped like a mermaid. "Wha-what? How did you turn into this..." she asked, looking horrified.

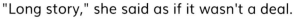

"Long story," she said as if it wasn't a deal.

"Please tell me the story!" she said uncomfortable about talking to sea foam.

"Alright, I'll tell you," said Ariel. "So I made a deal with the sea witch after marriage, she said that if I use this sabre to slice Prince Charming, I would stop being a sea foam, but of course, I couldn't go on land because I was a seafoam mermaid by then so I couldn't get revenge on Prince Charming."

Ana looked confused. "Oh alright, I'm a seafoam so I can't go on land!" she said. "I can watch things if they're close to the water, just like the Evil Queen."

Ana tilted her head even more confused. "Who is the Evil Queen?" she asked.

Ariel sighed. "Oh alright, she's the old queen that poisoned Snow White with that apple!" she said, looking again at Ana trying to not be confused.

"What was the power the Evil Queen had like yours?" she asked with 100 questions filling in her mind but one came out.

"Her power was looking through mirrors, but sadly she got sucked into one of her mirrors when her former love was gone, she is now living in mirrors at The Land of Stories, so no need to worry about her spying on you doing your make-up!" said Ariel, sighing. "Well it's already time for your bed so go on out with Shimmer Rose, take care!"

Ana went to her vacation home, looking after Rose, and went to her concert, trembling backstage.

Ana was about to leave in twenty-five minutes when, "Next up on stage! Anabelle Stan!"

Ana breathed as she walked onstage. "Hello! I am going to show you my newest design! Mermaid Gem!" she said.

"Oooooh ahhhh!" the audience squealed at the sequins shimmering along the stage.

"How much?" asked the producer.

"It's 65 baht, all right!" she said.

"How did you get the idea?" asked a little girl with a pearl in her hair and blonde hair.

"Well, little one, today I found a beautiful mermaid cave!"

The guards looked confused. "Umm, are you alright?" one of them asked her.

"Nevermind..."

She smiled backstage and pulled a fish out of her jeans, a cat appeared! Not just any cat... Shimmer Rose!

"Ohhhhhh, aaahhh!" everyone squealed happily...

"Wait! But you're an acrobat, not a designer!" screamed someone named Khao Tu from the crowd wearing a T-shirt with Khao Tu on it.

"Oh yeah!" Ana said. "Well, I guess we should start..."

At home, she was working on her laptop with her cat attacking the mouse playfully and Anabelle was working on her new essay when her cat turned into a ' red panda'. The red panda was shimmering just like her cat.

Ana slapped her head as the red panda meowed..."Silly little cat!"

Maki Puttal (9)

The American School Of Bangkok, Thailand

The Bear

Hi, my name is Miller, I'm a scientist. Right now, I have to go to Bear Island to explore caves, wildlife, water and temperature, all related to global warming.

While I was on the boat to go to Bear Island, Tar, the captain's boat son asked me, "Have you ever gone to Bear Island before?"

"No," I answered.

"You gotta be careful, there are walruses and it's very cold," Tar said.

"Land! Land!" said the captain.

"I gotta pack my things now," I told Tar.

Bear Island was full of ice. I walked to my cabin and unpacked my things. I found my daughter's pictures and tears rolled down my face. I missed her so much. It was my fault she died. I let her run on the road then a car came and it hit my daughter.

At night, I looked at the window, there was a thing that was bear-shaped. It couldn't be a polar bear, could it?

Tomorrow, I woke up so early and did my work. When I finished doing my work, I went outside and walked to where I saw the creature I saw last night, but there is no living thing. I just walked and walked until I was about three miles away from the cabin. That's when I saw a polar bear.

I froze, white-faced. The polar bear was so big. It roared the loudest thing I have ever heard. I looked at its whole body and that was when I figured out that it was so skinny for a polar bear and around its paw, there was a fishing net.

"Hello," I said. The bear replied with a roar.

I ran away home that time.

In the evening, I went back to where the bear was with a knife and two bags of biscuits and peanut butter.

"Hello," I said.

The bear replied with a roar.

"I mean you no harm, I'm just going to help you with your paw and I'm going to feed you."

I walked cautiously towards the bear. Its paws were so big. I cut carefully so the knife wouldn't cut the bear's skin.

After about thirty minutes of hard work, I finally managed to cut the net. The bear licked me. I laughed. "I should give you a name. Your name should be Bristle!" I gave Bristle my peanut butter and biscuits. It gobbled them up right away. I played with Bristle for a long time.

At 6:30am, it was time to go back to my cabin. "Wait for me here tomorrow, Bristle," I said.

When I go back to my cabin, I ate my dinner and went to sleep.

At 8:20am, I woke up and did my work. I packed up my peanut butter and biscuit into my pocket and went to where I met Bristle.

When I get there, Bristle was already there. "Hi!" I said.

The bear roared in reply. I gave Bristle my peanut butter and biscuits, then, something flashed in my mind. How did Bristle get to Bear Island because in the book, there are no polar bears left on Bear Island?

"How did you get here?" I asked, then the bear's eye started to look sad and it placed its snout on me and right away, I knew how Bristle came here by instinct like I could communicate with Bristle.

Bristle had moved here with his mother seven years ago, then her mother died here and the ice caps around Bear Island. That polar bear used to move to Svalbard (a country) melted. That's how Bristle was stuck here!

"Bristle, one day, I'll definitely move you to Svalbard," I said.

The next day, I woke up and called Tar to come to Bear Island and pick Bristle up.

When Tar arrived, his father was holding a gun, Bristle got shocked by the weapon and roared. Tar's father, shocked by the roar, aimed the rifle at Bristle and was about to shoot it when I stood in front of Bristle.

"Move!" Tar's father said. "I will kill the bear!"

"You can kill my bear, but you will have to kill me first!" I replied.

"And me," said Tar.

"Tar! What the heck are you doing?"

"The bear is dangerous, can't you see?" Tar's father shouted.

"Bristle isn't dangerous, she is only shocked, I could control her if you want."

"Well then, if you could, put him into my ship and into the cage," Tar's father said. "We're going to leave right now."

At the next day of travelling, the sea was so rough that I had to stay in my room and vomit.

"If the sea is rough like these for the whole journey, it would take about a week to reach Svalbard," Tar said.

"A week? I can't wait for a week, I have to do my work. I thought travelling from Bear Island to Svalbard only takes about two days?" I said.

"Yes but not on a rough sea like this," Tar replied.

"Get out of my room, I'm not feeling well," Tar went out of my room...

Three days later, the sea was not rough anymore. "It will only take about two more hours to reach Svalbard!" Tar's father said.

Two hours later, we arrived at Svalbard. Time to put Bristle to the wilderness. I went into Bristle's cage and sadly said, "Bristle, get out, you're now going to live in Svalbard."

I took Bristle to a shore on Svalbard. "I love you so much," I said, then, I got back to the boat and the boat moved.

I looked at Bristle, he was being smaller and smaller whenever the boat got farther. Then, when he was going to disappear, I shouted, "Bristle, I love you so much! I would never find a good friend like you ever again! Be healthy, I'm sure one day, we will meet again. Goodbye!"

Then, sadly, Bristle let out the biggest roar...

Patipol Dumrongchai (10)

The American School Of Bangkok, Thailand

The Cursed Swordswoman

A long time ago, in a forest in India, there was a mini swordswoman who was cursed by an evil witch. The evil witch was old and she was supposed to be cursed when she was 20 years old, but the curse didn't work. Now the witch was mad.

A year passed and then the curse worked. Now the swordswomen, Alia was cursed. Alia was a girl with brown, hazel eyes, dark brown thick hair, a few strands falling on her face, a thin body, and dark lovely skin. Alia loved to do gymnastics, dance and go to ninja practice.

Suddenly, Alia felt a wave of pain stab her. She felt herself get smaller and smaller. She saw all her clothes were ginormous. It felt like she got small or did the world get bigger? She thought about going to the Holy Priest. So she got in her yellow mini toy car and drove to the priest's house.

When she got to the priest's house and rang the doorbell. *Ding-dong!* screamed the bell which was right in her face. After a few minutes of ringing the doorbell, the priest came out and let her in. The priest looked very old, with a long beard and grey hair. He always wore a long gown which was as dark as the midnight sky, in fact even darker.

"Oh, Holy priest," cried Alia with tears falling down her cheeks as big as raindrops and as bitter as the salty ocean. "I have shrunk. Help me!"

"Oh my, only a wise old lady can help you, my dear!" said the wise old priest.

So a day passed, and in Alia's brain the priest's words were ringing in her mind like a whirlpool of fish. She thought about going to the old lady. Then she remembered a small emerald bracelet the priest gave her.

She got up and went to get it. It was covered in precious stones and gems. She wore it and got a bit bigger or was she seeing things?

She thought she was in her dreams. She needed to get to the old lady as soon as possible! She threw herself in the car and went to the old lady's house.

A few hours later she reached her house. The old lady welcomed her in. Alia told her about what had happened. The wise old lady told her to drink the yellowish potion at 12pm sharp. The old lady started to mumble some words. All of a sudden she said darkly, "Alia dear, this will cure you, this potion will cure you. And this my dear is a curse."

Alia stared after getting the potion. Then she backed away and ran. Her heart pounding she went into the yellow mini car and zoomed out of there.

For days and days, Alia had nightmares of the priest and the old lady. Then their words rang in her head. Then with a change of mind, she drank the yellowish potion. Then she got bigger. A wild spread of joy burst out... but it got darker and darker until it faded. She was now a giant.

She rushed back to the old lady panting. At first, the old lady was scared then she realised it was Alia. The old lady whispered through the window, "Why have you become a giant? The potion was supposed to work."

Alia replied with a pout that was literally reaching the road, "I do not know."

The old lady let out a long hoarse sigh and a loud mumble, "What time did you drink the potion?"

Alia replied, "At 11:59, did I do anything wrong? Was I supposed to drink it at 12:00 sharp?"

"Yes my dear, you were supposed to drink it at 12:00 sharp. This was dark magic and only time can cure you," grunted the wise old lady.

"Oh, I'm sorry that I didn't listen to your instructions. Is there another way for you to cure me?" cried Alia.

"Yes, my dear, there is a way. Now listen to me closely, you need to drink this potion at 12:00 sharp, I am repeating it again: 12:00 sharp then you will be cured." She gave Alia a green-blueish potion through the tiny rusty window.

Alia came home but stayed outside until it was 12:00. Then Alia remembered that she needed to drink the potion at 12:00 sharp. No mistakes!

When there were only ten minutes left to go, she got ready to drink the potion.

She checked her phone then a sound came from the phone, *buzz*. Then she realised it was 12:00. *Quickly*, she thought, *I have to hurry up before it's too late.*

She ripped the green-blueish potion out of the mini-sized bag and opened the cork as quickly as she could. When she took the cork out it made a plop sound. It fell in the river where she was sitting but she did not care. She just cared about getting to her normal size again.

When Alia was ready, she chugged until there was not even a single drop of the potion left.

She started to get smaller and smaller. A joy burst out but this time the joy remained! She was back to her normal size. The dark magic only worked when there was a full moon and only at 12:00. She was so happy. She ran back to the old lady's house and thanked her. Then she went back to her home and slept like a bear in winter.

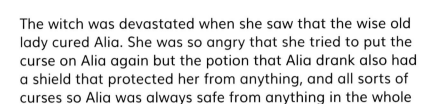

The witch was devastated when she saw that the wise old lady cured Alia. She was so angry that she tried to put the curse on Alia again but the potion that Alia drank also had a shield that protected her from anything, and all sorts of curses so Alia was always safe from anything in the whole wide world!

Avni Gupta (10)
The American School Of Bangkok, Thailand

Honey And Icy

Once upon a time, there was a mind-reading creature named Honey. She was a phoenix and had laser beam eyes. Honey was very smart and good at everything. She could read other people's minds.

One day, she woke up and saw a portal to another planet and went through it. The planet was a little crazy because there was a super giant alien and a super blue bright phoenix fighting each other!

Honey read the other phoenix's mind and he said, "I need help from another phoenix."

Then Honey went to the battle and shouted, "I will help you!"

Then, suddenly, the blue one said in his mind, "How did she read my mind? She must be a special one!"

She replied, "I am!"

After that, they told each other their names and the blue one's name was Icy, then they became friends and continued the battle.

Honey suggested, "Hey, how about I use my eyes?"

Icy replied, "Sure."

The two worked together and finally won the battle! Then Icy asked, "How did you get here?"

Honey responded, "I saw a portal in my room and it teleported me here." Icy pulled a weird face which confused Honey.

Then Icy understood and told Honey "That was my portal. I lost it years ago, do you know where it is?"

"No, sorry," stated Honey.

Icy said, "Honey, I have something to tell you, this planet is made out of pizza!"

Honey screeched, "Wow, perfect, now I'm hungry!"

Then Honey ate the whole planet and everyone was floating in space.

Honey saw another portal, so Honey teleported to another planet with Icy. Icy was super surprised to see this. Honey just teleported them to the fire world. Icy was so, so hot like he was breathing fire. Then Icy saw a glowing magical door, when he opened it there was an ice world behind the fire world!

Then Honey's wing was stuck in Icy's pocket and Icy just dragged Honey in the half-ice land so now Honey was freezing cold!

Honey said, "We need to go back!"

Icy added, "No! This is perfect, the other side is so hot!"

So now the two started fighting and Honey said, "I don't want to be friends with you now!"

Honey then magically magicked Icy back to space and Icy said before leaving the portal, "You'll regret this 100%, for sure!" but Honey just ignored him and he went back to space and never saw Honey again, ever again!

Honey went home and suddenly up in the sky was God telling Honey and Icy that they were brothers and sisters and Honey and Icy cried and ran to each other hugging and saying sorry.

The next day they lived together and Icy promised Honey, "I promise that I will never shout or yell at you ever again."

Honey said, "And I will stay with you forever!"
Years passed and they still stayed together but one day
they had a fight. "Forget what I said a few years ago, I hate
you icy!" shouted Honey.
Then they both went home crying to their old brothers and
sisters, Icy and Honey explained everything that happened.
Then Icy got powers from his parents, he could make people
fall in love!
When Icy was playing, he hit Honey's mom and Icy's dad
accidentally with his powers. They fell in love and Honey had
to stay with Icy forever. They both shouted,
"Noooooooooooooooooo!" and were always fighting about
whether they should live in Fire Land or Ice Land.
Then suddenly the clouds became a word and it spelt an
element. Then a bunch of colourful phoenixes were there
and Icy and Honey agreed to each have three element
phoenixes in their own gang to fight each other. "When
Mom and Dad are not here, for example, tomorrow Mom
and Dad will be at work!"
They fought with powers and, one day, when they were
fighting, they realised they were in the woods and they were
lost. They cried and cried but no one heard them.
Then one of Honey's elements said, "We have to survive!"
and Honey and Icy's element magicked them food and drink
to eat.
A few years passed and they survived. They were in the
forest and finally found their parents. They were still in love
so the four of them went home and the whole family
promised that they would stay together forever. Then they
lived happily ever after.

Rinlada Chaitrakulthong (9)

The American School Of Bangkok, Thailand

The Abandoned Forest

It's just me.

There is no danger. You can only hear the soft whistling from the wind and the old, cold sticks beneath you. Occasionally, above you can hear crows soaring but other than that it is silent. Whenever I'm there, every time I enter a fresh wave of air hits me. Whilst walking a natural old odour from the fallen logs, wanders around the forest air.

Above me, all I could see was dull, daunting, dangly fingers all intertwining with each other. Towering and peculiar; dusky and lanky; ancient and rugged, the trunks of the trees all stood still, quietly whispering to one another. Knowing that they had no rush, all the trees just sat there. Long, emerald-green vines climbed up the trees, slowly consuming each one. Bark crumbled off bit by bit, sticks snapped bit by bit, twigs fell bit by bit. Grey, desolated clouds covered the mysterious land every day, they all crept into the distance. It was a cycle. Everything that hit the forest grounds always got sunken deep into the forest floors and it never stopped going downwards.

Cool sensations flew through your fingertips and random shivers occurred in your spine. You could feel the world around you. Deep, dark, green moss grew up and down the trees and it sat on the rough, crackly bark. Rocks were plotted around places in the forest, they felt cold, lifeless and still. Each rock lay calm and admired the scenery of the land.

Most of the time your mouth is cold and dry but sometimes if you're lucky you can taste some of the natural leafy taste from the floors or other times that dull, boring taste creeps in. It's quite calming.

Freedom. You're free. A feeling of protection is there from all around. It's a bit bizarre but it's true.

Elif Stamcheva (12)
The Arnewood School, New Milton

Love Is Blind

Your voice: soft as the setting sun. My hands caress your face as if I was sculpting you from clay, for my eyes see only *darkness*; a perpetual agony. Lilly of the valley encapsulates your sweater (what a sweet scent it is).

Cupid has pierced me with his arrows, but I feel no pain, for the blood I bleed is my paint and our love my canvas, our fates entwined in a silly game we call life. My darling, you are the air that I breathe and without you a void is left in my heart. You have made me see in a different way - full of warmth and comfort. I do not require my vision to know of your beauty or kindness, your touch is enough.

Eleanora John (15)
The Heathland School, Hounslow

A Nocturnal Drive

The sun is stalking down the horizon; its blooming coral, pink and deep blue hues gently slipping into the descending void. The chatters of traffic have concluded their constant concert; although a few wisps of fuel continue to stain the silent air.

Nobody has claimed these streets. Nobody dares to ride under the stare of the stars. But some do, it's true. At this time of night, *the nocturnal thrive.*

The silence is broken by the thwack of wood against bone. A man flies backwards - landing on the pavement with a forceful thud. His assailant strides forwards - kicking his dagger away and under a nearby dumpster. She stares at his dazed face - hunting for any sign of activity. With a sigh, she then turned to face the observing shopkeeper. "Enjoyed the show?"

The unamused elder frowns. His eyes slide from the unconscious pickpocket, along the trail of red staining the ground, to the various smashed crates and bottles surrounding the girl's sneakers.

"Goddammit kid, you gotta learn to clean up your own messes."

"Will do sir!" the girl exclaimed.

"Although, I'm in a bit of a rush tonight..."

She kneels next to the body, rummaging through his coat. A jingling set of keys is plucked out. "No good thief!" She spits at his feet.

The girl juggles the keys as she struts away from the store. She turns left and disappears between a damaged chain-link fence. A single streetlight illuminates the tiny alleyway.

Her palm traces the metallic material of the motorbike. It reaches the handlebars, gripping their familiar surface as well as the precious keys. Her other fist clutches a baseball bat; which she slings over her shoulder. In a single movement, she hauls herself onto the worn seat and slams the key into the ignition. As soon as she turns it, the alley fills with a booming roar. Sheer power rumbles through the engine. With a gentle twist of the throttle- the bike lurches forwards.

After threading the gap in the fence, the bike began to accelerate. The girl could feel each crack and bump of the road. Nevertheless, the bike continued to shoot down the street - slicing the warm summer sky. Faster and faster. Surrounding buildings become a blur. Mechanical thunder is accompanied by the air's whistling. Above, the stars glimmer amongst a black sea. Life or death, the only warning is the road ahead.

Soon there is a strange absence of working street lamps. Everything is dark. Suddenly, a series of torch beams shine towards her; followed by a series of yelps alerting the girl to the figures in her path. Pedestrians!

She squeezes the brakes as the bike jerked to a halt.

"Argh, what the hell! Watch where you're going!"

Out of all the faces that gawked at her arrival, his seems the most irritated. Despite being quite young, the amount of stubble and scars he has suggested otherwise. A hot-headed leader of one of the many gangs who fought claim over the city's streets. He boasts a scuffed red tracksuit, brighter than any flag.

195

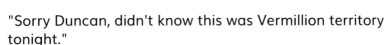

"Sorry Duncan, didn't know this was Vermillion territory tonight."

The girl hops off the motorbike and examines the rest of the crowd. Apparel of every colour seems to be present.

"Seems you got a few friends with you-"

His face grows almost as red as his outfit.

"You *dare* address me like that?" Duncan mutters. He steps forward. "After nearly running me over?"

Before she can reach for her bat, a much larger man (also clothed in red) grabs Duncan by the shoulder.

The man murmurs, "Boss, we don't gotta squabble with her..."

"Yeah! We got bigger problems right now!" a familiar voice exclaims.

They all turn to the woman emerging from a huge warehouse-like building. Even in the dark, her ruffled blonde hair and emerald eyes glint with agitation. She slams the door behind her and sprints through the crowd, her blue bandana flapping in the air.

After a moment of breathing, she nods towards the bat-wielding girl.

"Good to see ya, traveller." She then hastily looks at Duncan. "They've taken over the entire damn thing. And they don't wanna share an ounce of power with no one... unless we pay up."

Duncan's glare intensifies. "They think we'll surrender?" He glances at the crowd before turning his gaze back. "Val... you know we won't go down without a fight!"

The street is immediately filled with cheers.

Seeming satisfied, Duncan turns to the female biker,
"You better help us get those lights on, don't want another accident-"
The girl has already grabbed her bat and held it to the sky.
"If it's a brawl they want, it's a brawl they'll get!"

Darina Trujillo-Ravinger (15)
The Heathland School, Hounslow

My Brother

I realise that I don't talk much about my brother. Mainly, because he's always up in his room; playing on his PS4 or watching something on Netflix; our bond slowly wilting away by the minute but then strengthening whenever we'd have a conversation. Our connection, like an indecisive see-saw.

When I was younger, my brother was the closest person to me, he was practically my best friend growing up. Whenever he wanted to go outside or go to the neighbour's house to play football with them, I'd always tag along. Considering the fact that there weren't many girls I knew in my area; the people my brother played with were all boys, and combined with my exuberance as a young child and how susceptible I was to injuring myself, I had tough skin (literally).

My older sister/cousin and I have an 18-year age gap (I know, *big* age gap). My 2nd older sister and I have a 5-year age gap and my brother and I have a 4-year age gap. My older sister/cousin was already married by the time I was born. My 2nd sister was always interested in doing her own thing and being a 'lone wolf', whereas, my brother would (most of the time) include me in the things he did. To this day, my brother and I still have the classic sibling duo; always teasing each other and joking around. Nevertheless, he isn't perfect. But then again, who is?

He can be quite sardonic at times and rather incompetent when it comes to doing tasks around the house; so much so that my sister and I often have to rectify and correct his mistakes and the cut corners. Sometimes, we fight and practically jump at each other's throats. I sometimes wish that he wasn't around or even existed.

Even though he is up in his room 24/7 and it's like he doesn't exist, his presence is made known to anyone who's in the house because of his persistent grunts and screams of joy when watching a football match in his room. It's times like those I wish I could jump at his throat and shut him up for good.

But would I still have the same life I do now? Would I have even learned how to play FIFA without my brother? Would I even be me?

So, I should talk more about my brother because, at the end of the day, he has got to be one of the weirdest people I know, and begrudgingly, love.

Aamina Nor Mohammed (15)

The Heathland School, Hounslow

My Last Letter To You

I loved you.
I loved you to the moon and back.
Heck, I loved you, through all the galaxies and for as long as there are stars.
I couldn't have imagined anything more or less than that. That unfathomable and outrageous feeling; that neither of us could've given into. We had tried and tried, yet failed. Maybe in some other life, we said to ourselves, knowing our hope was never going to save us.
I still remember when we had first met, that frosty winter day, where time had stopped, where we had found some love. I remember your hair being frozen and your bright blue eyes somehow more vibrant. I remember your touch and your smile and how you made that cold day a little bit warmer. I hadn't known at that point who you would've ended up being for me; I wish I had. Perhaps if I knew then, I wouldn't have stayed.
I remember our first conversation and how I was so harsh towards you, yet you wouldn't give up trying to talk to me and kept making sure I wouldn't forget you. I wish you hadn't because if you hadn't we wouldn't have been here now.
We wouldn't be trying to save ourselves from the what-ifs and maybes because we both know it's killing us; knowing that if we had tried a little harder or talked a little more maybe we would've gotten somewhere but we didn't.
So here I am, alone and wondering who you and I are, here I am hoping that everything will somehow work out, here I am knowing that there is no way we could go from being you and I to us. Just know that no matter what I will always love you.

Heck, I love you through all the galaxies and for as long as there are stars,
I love you to the moon and back.
I love you... and I don't think I could ever stop.

Kannan Singh (15)

The Heathland School, Hounslow

The Conundrum

I was in a conundrum,
A conundrum it was,
I did not know how to describe it
For I didn't know what it was,
But then I met you,
And you made it worse,

You were sitting in the darkness,
Waiting to converse,
That's when I found you.
I didn't think it was true,
For I didn't know it was you,

I don't think I ever met a girl that looked so blue,
You didn't look sad, but lost,
A bit mad and cross,
You rose to your minuscule height,
And our eyes met with an expression not so delight,
I think you hated me at first,
I admit, I felt the same too,
But I guess with time,
I felt different about you

Your company does not vex me so,
So, I stopped describing you as a dumb potato,
I do not know how it started,

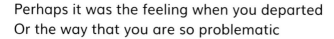

Perhaps it was the feeling when you departed
Or the way that you are so problematic

You were in the darkness,
When I found you,
So I stayed in the darkness with you
But now, the light seems to have beamed through,
And I knew it was true,
It had always been you,

I am in a conundrum.
A conundrum it is,
I do not know how to describe it,
Even though I know what it is.

I couldn't believe it was true
To have a conundrum like you.

Dhriti (15)
The Heathland School, Hounslow

Betrayed

She said her final words and left, there was no turning back time now. Her face said it all. She was serious, she'd left for good. I sank to the pavement beneath me; tears filling my eyes, clouding my vision softly and making the lights around me blur into a rainbow of warmth.

She'd left me in the cold winter park for a man she'd never met. A man. I felt betrayed that her love had wandered from the fairer sex, that she had lied about loving solely me. About loving only women.

I had tried to get her to marry me, but the priests at the church would never have allowed it. Not now, and I fear not ever.

Daisy Templeton (16)
The Heathland School, Hounslow

The World Around Us

The world around us is great but
Some things don't last forever.
We take things for granted but
With all our lives they should be cherished.

The shiny blue sea filled with bettas and turtles,
Cod and salmon.
And on the land we fertilise soil for our own lives.

We hunt for meat and we create new things,
Each and every day is a new opportunity to explore.

From as high as the clouds to the depths of the sea,
There are still many things we are yet to see.

From shimmering treasures to mystical beasts,
We will rest watching the golden sunset whilst relaxing
our feet.

Dancing daffodils queue along a green mile,
Above us are stars shining like disco lights,
Watching us dance into the night.

Jakob Holloway (12)
The King's CE School, Kidsgrove

The World

The world is in a terrible state.
They think it's a game but it's our world.
God made peace but we replaced it with war,
God made dreams we made nightmares,
He made birds music we made gunshots,
Gunshots made explosions,
God made friends we made loneliness,
God made life, we made suicide,
God made happiness, we made depression,
God made us, we killed others.
God made the world.
We destroyed the world.

Liam Whitehead (12)
The King's CE School, Kidsgrove

The Great Blue Ocean

Golden sand turns into liquid
When the baby blue ocean waves hit the shore.
Seashells wash up from the light sea floor.
The ocean breeze blows my hair into my face making
my hair messy
I think to myself about:

Climate change destroying the ocean and
Everything around it.
I also think about all of the sea creatures
Not being saved because of plastic.
Why would a human do such a thing?

Elizabeth Vaughan (12)
The King's CE School, Kidsgrove

The World Around Us

The world around us
What a sight to see!
Where the birds flee

The world around us
What a place to be.

The world around us
With all the bees, collecting their honey.

The world around us is
The best place to be.

Bethany Beech (12)
The King's CE School, Kidsgrove

The Bizarre Magic Show

We had Mr Flinch first period, we were learning about WWI. I wasn't concentrating and was looking out the window while my friend Steve was very focused because he loved history. The bell finally rang and the period was over.

We had break after English and we met up with Jack and Mark who are also my friends. Mark was holding a flying in his hand and I asked him what it was and he said it was an invitation for a magic show happening in town. We decided to check it out. Steve said he would buy the tickets.

The next morning, we were waiting for Steve to arrive with the tickets. At break, he told us that he was only able to buy two tickets due to some rules. We decided Steve was going for sure because he bought the tickets.

I had an idea, where Steve threw the ticket in the air and whoever caught it could go to the show.

We did exactly what we planned. Steve chucked it in the air and I could see the ticket glaring at my eyes. So I quickly jumped to get the tickets. Sure enough, I did. I was very happy because I'd never been to a magic show before.

The show was Saturday at 5pm. Me and Steve walked to the place and reached there at 4:45pm. It was a very tall building near the city centre. There were around 200 seats and quite a lot of people.

The spotlight turned on and the performer came onto the stage. His name was the Snake Boy. He started introducing himself, saying that he was born with a rare condition that made his skin and bones flexible. He bent backwards and crawled like a spider, covering his face with skin from his neck and doing other impossible turns and bends. The Snake Boy didn't spend much time on stage.

The spotlight turned off so the next performer could come on stage. The performer's name was Two Belly Chunk. He said he was born with two stomachs and could digest almost anything. He had a plate full of metal rods, screws, nuts, bolts, glass etc. He ate it like it was nothing and even ate the plate and digested it. Me and Steve were flabbergasted by the performer.

The light went off again and it looked pitch-black when the next performer came on stage. It was a fat lady dressed in a teeth outfit which looked weird. Her name was Gertha Ortha. She claimed that she had the strongest tooth in the world. She called three men with hammers and tools and checked if they were real.

After they confirmed they were real, she started eating them and spat them out. The hammer and the other tools looked like scrunched-up paper. Me and Steve were shocked. The lights went off again while we were thinking bout the lady. The final performer came and it was the Nailing Lady. Apparently, she could grow nails up to six feet in fifteen seconds. She closed her eyes, blocked her nose and tickled her chin. The nails started rapidly growing and she challenged the audience that no one could cut them. Loads of people tried sawing them, cutting with garden shears, or even a katana but everyone failed. It kept growing. She tickled her chin again and the nails went back to normal. That was the end of the show and me and Steve were very satisfied and shocked by the performers. We were talking about the show while walking home.

The next day we told Jack and Mark and they were surprised as well. We will definitely go again together if it comes back to town.

Mohnish Govindarajan (12)

The Westwood Academy, Canley

Dream On

I woke up to the melody of the birds. My curtains danced as the wind flowed around my room. The carpet snow outside mesmerised the whole neighbourhood. I sprang myself out of bed with pure excitement, knowing that it was two days before Christmas. I glanced at the clouds surfing across the blue sky.

Dancing my way down the stairs I caught a whiff of the most wonderful breakfast in the whole entire world. Fresh-picked berries sat on top of the spongy pancakes as the syrup drizzled down the pancakes.

I lived with my mother, who is an amazing cook, for most of my life. My dad left and never came back when I was a baby boy. Every birthday wish, every Christmas wish, I wished for my dad.

I slid into my chair getting ready to dig in but there was a strange knock on the door. I dashed straight to the door thinking it was a Christmas gift. I opened the door with such excitement just to see a strange man hiding in his own shadows. He handed me an important-looking letter addressed to my mom. I gave it to my mom with excitement. My mother opened it with joy thinking it was a gift. When she looked at it she froze in shock. I dug into her hands and glared at the envelope.

We had been evicted...

I packed my bag with despondency to leave. We said all our goodbyes to the neighbourhood. We dragged ourselves across the cobbled pavement in despair. A few minutes later, which felt like days, we found a bus stop. I looked at my mother and cried, "What will we do Mom?"

She looked at me and said, "Josh, we will be fine, do not worry."
One hour passed by and out of nowhere my mom had a terrifying heart attack. I had no idea what to do. I froze in utter shock.
I was alone. I was abandoned.
Two years passed and I was barely surviving in this wretched world. I lived in this fractured shack covered with all sorts of bugs. The dark greenery slowly started to consume the shack.
Suddenly, I heard it. It was coming from the other side of the shack. My shadow stalked me as I crept around the corner. The floorboard creaked so loud it sounded like bones cracking. My legs trembled. When I touched the slim door it sent a cold sensation through my veins.
My body tingled with curiosity. "What is behind that door?" I questioned myself.
When I opened the door, the curtains blew into my face. The bright light of the sun blinded my eyes. When my eyes started to adjust to the light I slowly started to realise the light, not the sun, was something much more amazing.
It was bright! It was mesmerising! It was a figure of light!
Suddenly, something came closer to me which looked like an angel. As I froze, my hair stood like soldiers and it also felt as if my soul abandoned me. Its bright yellow halo ring spun graciously as the white clothes glistened in the shadows.
"H-h-hello, who are you?" I whispered.
"I'm the one and only McFillieus McFurbeen from the Galactic Universe!"

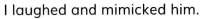

I laughed and mimicked him.

"This is no time to mess about, you my friend are in grave danger!" he bellowed.

"How am I in danger? I am just a regular ten-year-old boy."

"No my son, you will seek great help!" his deep voice announced.

"What help? I do not need help. Tell me!" I eagerly shouted.

"No time to explain. Be careful, he is almost here... you have been warned!"

Then out of thin air he vanished.

So many questions, yet so few answers.

As I left the isolated room I walked on the creaking floorboard to stumble on a pebble. A mysterious pebble. What could this mean...? I would soon find out.

The whole entire day I was wondering what McFillieus was talking about but I was also flustered about the rock. As soon as I got ready to go to sleep on my mouldy bed, I chucked my pebble across the floor thinking it was utterly useless.

Then, silence. *Bang!*

A mysterious light started flashing from the pebble. *What is this?* I thought to myself. So many miraculous and weird things happened today. The pebble got bigger and bigger as it flew higher and higher. My mouth gaped in amazement. The pebble suddenly spun around me in circles until it miserably dropped to the floor.

I went to go sleep and whispered to myself, "I wish for some food."

"Your wish is my command," a stranger whispered to me.

I looked around to see if McFillieus was fooling with me but no, the strange and mysterious voice came from the pebble. I got up with some curiosity and slowly walked over to the pebble.

Shaking nervously like a leaf, I touched the rock and food came pouring down. Chicken, steak, pork, pancakes, waffles and all kinds of fruits. Still having no clue, I curiously took hold of the pebble and another strange figure showed up but this time he was hiding in the shadows.

This strange figure bellowed, "Who dares to interrupt my sleep!"

I stubbornly replied, "You actually ruined my sleep you fool."

"Well, it is not my fault you wished for something."

I stood in pure confusion.

I saw the food and tried to smell it but could only smell waffles.

Suddenly I woke up and was still in shock. My mom was shaking me and telling me, "Wake up Josh, wake up. You're late for school." I shot right up and looked around. I saw my mom, my normal bedroom and I also smelt the luxurious waffles downstairs sitting in the kitchen. I glared at my mom and I quickly went for a hug. She looked at me and chuckled softly.

I was relieved that it was a dream.

Aati Sivamyooran (12)
The Westwood Academy, Canley

My Parents

God's most beautiful creations are parents and we exist in this world as a result of them. They gave birth to us and all we have today resulted from them. There is no one else in the world like parents, they are the most significant individuals in our life. More than everything else in the world my parents love me. They frequently don't communicate their affection in words but we can immediately tell when they do. Most dads rarely show their love for their kids in words but they care about us more than they do about themselves. Mothers on the other hand show love through all they do. They deserve the same love and respect that we do therefore we must also respect and love them.

They instruct us on all we need to know as children including how to eat, walk, speak and play. Our parents have given us all we've ever needed to be happy ever since the day we were born. They groom us to give us the best they can despite their daily struggles. To give us access to food, education, clothing and all of our favourite things they sacrifice their comforts, their dreams and even their most prized possessions.

They put in a lot of effort for us and devote their entire lives to improving our lives and providing us with a comfortable existence. Because of this, we see our parents as the living God.

I also help my mom clean plates, wash, and cut vegetables. I help her clean the room's furniture and the entire house. I help my father with marketing and cleaning bikes. Furthermore, I go with him to the market and assist him in buying things.

In this manner, I like to help my parents whenever they need me. Our parents gave us birth; it is because of them that we came into this world. Everything that we are today is because of our parents. They are surely our living God.
Our parents love us more than anything else in this world. They teach us to live and dedicate their lives to giving us a healthy and nourishing lifestyle. From the day of our birth, they serve us with everything they can. They give us food to eat and provide us with an education, clothes and all our basic needs. My mother makes breakfast for me as soon as I wake up and she makes sure that my school bag, my uniform, and all my other items are prepared to go to school. My father goes with me to school early in the morning and at noon when school is over he comes to pick me up. I help my mom and dad with all their daily activities. My mother and father have a powerful impact on my life; they help me make important decisions and change my thoughts.
The significance of love affection and obligations to our parents is also reflected in our Pakistani culture. This implies that our parents are as much as God. Without a question, parents care deeply about their children. In a similar way, my parents adore me dearly. Every morning my mother serves my favourite breakfast and then she makes me get ready for school. She provides me with wholesome food as soon as get home. She also gives me snacks in the evenings and occasionally makes me a special dinner. She cares for me all day long and shows her affection for me.
On the other hand, my father guides me and teaches me basic things about our world society and other important knowledge. He encourages me to do things and helps me to achieve my targets. He also loves me a lot.

217

Both my mother and father are very active individuals. To make the day go on the labour gruellingly. My mother makes breakfast for the whole family in the early morning hours. She then occupies herself with additional housework. She feeds me looks after my clothes and cleans my shoes, school uniform and other belongings. She makes certain that everything I own is organised and spotless.

She also sees to it that I have a healthy lifestyle and am in good physical shape by providing me with a cup of warm milk each evening. On his way home my father picks up my favourite ice cream for me. He helps me finish my schoolwork while simultaneously playing with me. He instructs me and helps me in memorisation things I learned in school. This way they help me in all my daily activities.

A role model is someone who has a significant influence on our lives and who modifies the way we think and act. My parents are the first people that spring to mind when I consider myself a role model. They fulfil all the requirements for good parents. They are responsible and devoted to their work. They are committed to ensuring that we have a promising future. They may not be perfect ever but they do possess all the traits and values necessary to be successful parents. I assist my parents with a variety of various tasks. I quickly dressed after waking up and helped my mother in the kitchen while she prepared breakfast very busy with their daily activities but they still find time for me my brother and they spend time with us.

I love to be with my parents as they are very loving and caring and they understand me better than anyone else. I love my parents very much and they too love me a lot. And everyone should be grateful because when our parents die we won't have them so be grateful.

Conclusion:

Everyone loves their parents because they help them and protect them from many evils in this world. Our parents not only protect us and guide us on the right path but they also make a lot of sacrifices for our well-being.

I cannot describe the value that my parents have in my life. I am blessed that I had such a beautiful loving and caring father and mother.

Joan Hussain (12)

The Westwood Academy, Canley

The Unexpected

Me and my dad rushed onto the orange-painted aeroplane and we hurried into our seats. I sat next to the window and next to my dad, so I could see the beautiful scenery of the world's nature from high above.

The seats on all rows were filled. I felt slightly anxious and nervous as it was my first time flying but all of the fear went away as my dad reassured me by holding hands with me and comforting me.

Moments later the pilots were giving safety precautions and what to do if we were in danger. That moment a feeling of fear travelled down my back, and also said take off will be in a few minutes. I felt safe with my dad's company.

The plane slowly started to move. I held my dad's hand as tight as possible. My ears popped, my head slowly started to spin but it went away in seconds. I felt something warm on my right side cheek, it felt like a hot beautiful kiss but it was the blistering beautiful sun. We were in the air ready to go on a holiday. I was excited!

I looked outside and my eyes were blessed by the stunning view. The beautiful scenery like a blossoming garden. The different rays of the sun through the clear evening sky. The golden dusty sun was like a heart on the horizon in the clear view ahead. Tiny segments of dust dancing around in the evening night at the comfy pillow-like clouds guarding us while we were on the plane. Glistening stars of luminescence filled the crevasse of the clouds. I could see from a far distance. The electric blue ocean swiftly swaying in the wind in the night. The waves crashing into another, it was very peaceful. It felt like I was in heaven, everything was its own comforting symphony...

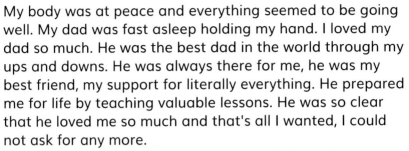

My body was at peace and everything seemed to be going well. My dad was fast asleep holding my hand. I loved my dad so much. He was the best dad in the world through my ups and downs. He was always there for me, he was my best friend, my support for literally everything. He prepared me for life by teaching valuable lessons. He was so clear that he loved me so much and that's all I wanted, I could not ask for any more.

If my dad was happy then I was happy, his happiness meant a lot more than my happiness. There was no one in this world I would love more than my dad. He always stuck up for me and made sure I was safe. This is why I love him so much.

In this plane there were quiet chatters and the small giggles of the children were heard and altogether they made a loud song, but that all silenced my mind as my dad was holding my hand with so much love and because of the beautiful scenery my eyes were blessed with. I was just thinking about the future, the memories that will be made on this holiday. It was all white when I looked out the window, it felt like heaven. In the background I saw the beautiful pointy mountains. If I looked on top of the window I could see white dots in the sea chirping and flying and surrounding the flight like our personal bodyguards.

Moments later the plane had a beeping sound and it alarmed everyone in the whole plane. The pilot exclaimed, "Dear ladies and gentlemen we are experiencing a high level of turbulence right now, thanks." I looked out at the wing next to me. One of the engines was smoking and it was dancing around.

Suddenly oxygen masks fell from the roof, flight attendants came in and helped. I made sure we both put our oxygen masks on securely. There were thoughts flooding in my head at that moment. There was panic in this whole plane. Me and my dad were in fear for our lives. I was scared even to look around. I was just praying that my dad would be safe. I hoped this was a dream but unfortunately I knew it wasn't. The plane was completely out of control, there was nothing to do except to hope for the best. All the passengers had lost hope. We kept hugging each other. I prayed to God I could see another day but it was not promising at all. Everyone was screaming their voices off in the plane. There was now a huge flame. Three-quarters of the plane was now lit on fire towards the back. We all knew we were going to die at this point, no one really had any fate. I lost all hope in myself. I accepted my unfortunate fate...

The plane ended up submerging in the cold snow and then the plane crashed on the mountains. I opened my eyes and everyone was just lying on the floor. Everyone was bloody from head to toe including me. There were many innocent passengers and lives on this flight. I was trapped beneath the wing and I could not move my neck.

I scanned around looking for my dad but I could not see him. My heartbeat was fast. I could only hear faint cries of all the innocent passengers exclaiming, "What did we do to deserve this?"

I crawled on my knees looking for my dad whilst suffering in unbearable agony. I saw someone with a similar T-shirt my dad wore. I crawled towards it and it was my dad. My body was filled with sadness. All I could see was a skeleton and pieces of glass stuck in his body.

His shoulders were somewhere and his arms were somewhere. He was out of place. He was not a human anymore. Everything was gone. I felt empty, I felt heartbroken. I wish I died instead of him.

Abbylan Roshan (12)
The Westwood Academy, Canley

A Child Of Echoes

The crunch of a leaf. The snap of a twig. I spun, knife in hand, I sprinted forward. Something or someone had found me. The cool morning air hit me as I ran. I had to get out of there. The patter of feet behind me told me that I was being followed. I made a sharp turn in the direction I believed to be the one I had come from. Then it hit me. I was a fool, leading the mortal to my safe spot.

Whizz. An arrow flew past me, only inches away from my shoulder. Whoever this imbecile was, they were armed. Out of the corner of my eye, I saw several other arrows follow the last. I continued to flee. There was no point in fighting back. My head throbbed. I could hardly bear it. I had to get back. I twisted round and hurled my knife, hoping to distract the person. I heard a screech from behind. This was my chance to get away.

I clambered through the vines and into my cave. The place that I called home. My stomach growled. I hadn't been able to catch any grub. I yanked off my worn boots and threw them to the side. It was time to get some rest.

I woke suddenly. Judging by how dark it was, it was still night-time. It was only then that I noticed the throbbing pain in my head. But why? There was nobody nearby. Or was there? I scrambled up off of the floor and grabbed the last remaining knife from my bag. I clutched it tightly. I made as little sound as possible as I tiptoed towards the entrance.

I crouched and peered through the vines. It was dim outside and near impossible to see. All was silent until...

"Do you think we are in the right place?" said a deep voice.
"The tracks stop here," said another.
Shoot! I had forgotten to cover my tracks. I had been too busy running away from the person. My head throbbed more intensely the closer they got. "Argh!" I cried. Then I heard leaves rustling followed by a voice.
"Over there, that way!" I had blown my cover. It was time to get out of here. I went inside and grabbed my backpack. Then I ran.
"Hey, come back!" screamed one of the voices.
"Freeze, elf!" said the other.
I kept going. I heard the footsteps of the two men close behind me. I knew they would not stop until they caught me, or I was dead.
Elves had been extinct for centuries until one day. When I was born, everything seemed normal, other than the fact I was an albino, until I reached the age of three. I began to develop pointy ears.
My parents began to worry and later discovered that I was an elf. Nobody knew how this was possible as, like I said, they went extinct long ago. Or so they thought.
After the discovery, life was different for us. We went into hiding. Elves were seen as a threat to humans and I was wanted dead. I grew up in an old,
abandoned house that badly needed repairing and all was well until I was nine.
Me and my father had been out catching food all night. We were tucking into our freshly caught grub when we heard talking nearby. My mother and father shared a worried expression. My mother grabbed my arm and looked deep into my eyes.

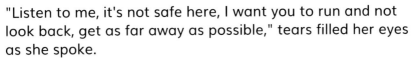

"Listen to me, it's not safe here, I want you to run and not look back, get as far away as possible," tears filled her eyes as she spoke.

"But-" I started. *Whizz!* A dagger whizzed towards me. I heard it before I saw it and ducked out of the way. However, my father didn't and it hit him right in his temple. He shrieked as blood trickled down his face. I screamed as I watched him drop to the ground, lifeless.

"Run!" my mother begged me.

I grabbed my bag with what little things I had and I did as told. I ran as fast as I could. Away from my lifeless father. Away from the dangerous people. I heard another shriek that I believed had come from my mother but I didn't look back. Tears streamed down my face as I fled. My only hope was to get away from this place. As far as possible. And that's how I ended up here. In this very wood. The furthest I could get before I was too tired to go any further. And this is where I have stayed for five years.

Using my father's hunting skills to stay fed and my mother's camouflage tactics to stay hidden. Never had anyone been close to finding me and I had begun to think that they had forgotten about me. I had been a fool.

I tore through the forest, trying to escape the terrors within. The men followed closely behind. Why me? Why couldn't I just be normal like everyone else? Why couldn't I just be left alone? That's all I wanted, a normal life.

"What do you want from me!" I asked, still running.

"You know exactly what we want, little girl."

"I don't!" I replied honestly. "Just leave me alone!"

"Silly girl, why should we do that?"

"Because I'm not a threat to you!" The men laughed slyly and continued to chase me. Why couldn't they just listen? All I wanted is to live a good life. Not one where I was constantly in terror.

I had been running for what felt like years and daylight was emerging. I was beginning to feel exhausted whereas the men weren't showing any sign of fatigue.

My feet were sore and hunger clawed at my stomach. I still couldn't see the edge of the forest, even after hours and I was beginning to think it would never end...

Autumn Jones (11)

The William Allitt School, Newhall

Pepper Travels To An Island

Date: 21st April 2048

One afternoon Pepper was reading a book. He heard his doorbell ring. He opened the door and saw Mole there.

"Let's go to an island," said Mole.

"Which island?" asked Pepper.

"Parrot island," spoke Mole.

"You mean the island which we saw on the posters?"

"Yes, that one!"

"Is anyone coming with us?"

"No, only the two of us."

"How long does it take to get there?" asked Pepper.

"It's a good 300km from here, so by a normal ferry, it will take 10 hours, but by a seaplane ferry, about an hour." You're referring to the sky hotel (big plane) that launched in 2034. It was too expensive. I'd rather take a regular ferry."

"No, silly, it's not the sky hotel. It's the Nuke supercharger-49. It is a seaplane with four decks. It costs 20,000 for an adult."

"Okay. That's reasonable."

"I think we can go."

"First, I booked a ticket myself, but I have a bonus ticket. You can have it, declared Mole. "We must get to the docks by 14:30."

"What time is it?" asked Pepper.

"13:50."

"We need to get moving soon."

They took the port bus and arrived at the docks.

Then they boarded the seaplane.

They stayed in their cabin. They talked, ate, and had fun.

The steward was Mole's cousin's sister's husband. He was very kind. Additionally, he has some exciting information about Parrot Island.

For example: "Do you know that Parrot Island was created in 2023 and that originally it was a tiny island with only white foxes living there?" said the steward.

"Oh, we didn't know that," replied Mole and Pepper in unison.

After the steward left, they were still speaking.

"I hope there is a lodge over there," Pepper said.

"There is one. I booked it," said Mole.

They reached the island.

"Wow, it's pretty huge," said Pepper.

"Let's go to the lodge," said Mole.

"Yup."

They reached the edge of a shore.

They saw a cluster of huts on a teeny-weeny island nearby.

"Man, it's approximately 100m away," said Mole.

"Do we have to swim? I haven't swum in a long time," spoke Pepper.

"It's pretty deep."

"I see a wooden kayak."

Hey, I saw it too."

"Let's ride."

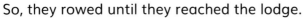

So, they rowed until they reached the lodge.

When they got to the lodge, they met Star and Kevin, who were good old friends.

They introduced themselves, "I am professor Kevin, the CEO of STR."

"I am an English, history and geography teacher at Golden Apple International School," said Star. "I am terrible at biology, so don't expect me to answer animal questions."

The next day, they set out to observe the southern part of the island.

"Do you like Minecraft? It is such a nice game..." rambled Star.

"Button your mouth already. We are not playing video games right now!" scolded Kevin.

Pepper suddenly heard a noise from an orange bush.

"What was that?" asked Pepper.

A pig appeared from the bush.

"Oink, oink, snort, snort," sniffed the pig.

"It's just a hogli-I mean a pig," said the star.

"B-but wild pigs are ferocious. They can kill a human by ripping them apart," said Kevin.

"Nah. These pigs were accidentally released here. They keep the island in check," said Mole.

"Let me take a photo," said Pepper.

The pig turned its back and ran off.

"Aww. I wanted to take a photo," grumbled Pepper.

"Don't worry, more pigs are on this island," Kevin explained.

"Hey, why are there so many different coloured parrots around here?" asked Pepper.

"Actually, parrots, pigs, and cats were introduced to this island," said Kevin.

"He is right. Once, this was a one-acre island full of white foxes. Now humans have made it much larger and introduced animals. Now it measures 17 acres. It was told to me by my steward cousin," said Mole.

"There are even natural hybrid parrots such as Camelot macaws and Catalina macaws," explained Kevin.

"Oh, is that true?" Pepper gasped.

"Yeah, yeah, boring information," yawned Star.

"You shouldn't have come here in the first place," muttered Kevin.

"I only came here for sightseeing," Star said.

They explored more of the south part of the island and then returned to the beautiful small lodge.

The next day they set out to observe the north part of the island.

"Supercalifragilisticexpialidocious!" sang Star.

"What was that for?" asked Mole.

"It is the longest word. People will think you are a smart guy if you say that," responded Star.

"Shut up; you'll flush the birds away," Kevin hissed back.

"Down the toilet?" asked Star.

"Uggh!" moaned Kevin.

They heard a bark.

"Hey, I see a white fox," Pepper nearly shouted.

Kevin responded, "Albino foxes are common around here."

"Yeah, there are cats too on this island," said Mole.

"You said that already, plus I thought they were all ocelots and tiger cubs," said Star.
"Are you mad? Tiger cubs live with their mother!" Kevin roared.
Kevin walked forward, and suddenly he fell into a pit.
Everyone rushed to see him.
"Are you okay?" said Mole.
"Yes, I am alright, only a slight scratch. That's all," said Kevin
"It looks like a pig dug it," said Mole
"Give me the lantern," said Kevin.
Pepper tossed the torch into Kevin's hand.
"Hey, I see a hole," said Kevin
He wanted to know where it led.
He crawled through the hole and finally came out through another hole.
"It looks like the pig got stuck, so it dug its way out. Pigs are intelligent," declared the professor.
So, they continued exploring until they got tired. They even found a fish fossil.
Finally, it was time to leave.
The seaplane arrived.
Pepper and his pals boarded the seaplane.
They all shared the same cabin.
"Hey, I found an orphaned parrot chick," spoke Star.
"Keep it and raise it for five months and release it back into the wild," grumbled Kevin as he drifted off to sleep.
When they reached the docks, Pepper and Mole said farewell to Star, the professor and Kevin. They all headed home.

Aaramudhan Chandrasekaran (10)
Tokyo Bay International School, Tokyo

232

Santa's Cookies

2015, December 24th,
I would get everything I could to make Santa Claus happy.
Since I would give him the best cookies from my snack bar,
it was my big chance to get the most presents from him.
Well, at least for now, it was 9:00 in the evening, and I
couldn't go to bed because of a lack of cookies. So I set my
timer to 2:00 in the morning, and sure enough, *riiiiiiing!*
shouted the alarm. Luckily, Santa wasn't around.
I had good news, bad news, and horrible news. Good news:
My parents were in a deep sleep so they couldn't hear the
alarm. Bad news: I needed to pass my parent's room to get
the cookies. Horrible news: The maid we hired a month ago
woke up to see what was coming up with that sound.
She rushed to my room. "What's the problem, kid?" asked
the maid.
I told her the whole story and promised not to tell my
parents. She promised. "What a relief," I said.
I walked. I sneaked. I looked. And there it was, the cookies. I
ate half of the cookies and then did the opposite process. I
looked. I sneaked. I walked.
After that, I slept. I woke up at 10 in the morning. Mom was
waiting for me to wake up, and she was not happy.
"What is that brown stuff on your mouth," she growled.
I wiped my mouth and replied, "Nothing."
Mom knew I was lying, so she said I couldn't watch my
favourite TV show for a solid month. Probably she could get
over this in three days or so.

Sushant Poudel (12)
Tokyo Bay International School, Tokyo

233

Whodunnit?

I went to the reception of Hotel Parco. A short bald man with a long crooked nose was tiredly standing. He was the manager of the hotel. I desperately asked, "Is Robbie here?" "Mr Robbie is at his home," he answered with his high-pitched British accent.

I thanked him, heading off to Robbie's house. Robbie, my best friend, is a 35-year-old fair man with a long beard. His fat nose stretches up to two inches.

I arrived at his two-story mansion, finely bricked with a lavish design. I rang the bell a few times, but no one was there to answer. I tried knocking, but the door was already open.

Everything seemed a little different and displaced inside. I could hear nothing but my footsteps. I felt as if someone was watching me from the first floor. I walked up the stairs. "Robbie! Where are you? I've come to meet you," I called out. My voice faintly echoed through the mansion.

I opened the door of his bedroom, searched the cupboard, and saw two almond-shaped eyes with thick eyebrows. It pushed me, and I immediately ran away. I tried plunging his broad shoulders while chasing him. Finally, he was trapped in the corner, but before I pulled out my gun, I got hit with a rod on my head.

After some time, I found myself on a chair and felt severe pain in my head. My blurred vision slowly came back. I saw my senior police, Mr. Hill, and my juniors, Maria and James. Beside my chair, I saw Robbie lying in a pool of blood. Tears welled up in my eyes and rolled down my cheeks, causing my throat to close.

I screamed, "Robbie! I promise that I'll find out who did this to you!"

"What are you talking about? You killed your friend and now you're lying," my senior, Mr Hill, screamed. He picked me off the ground and shoved me into the police car. His thin eyebrows joined, creating lines on his forehead. Whenever I'd try explaining, he would ignore me and yell, "Give your excuse in jail!" I was kept in a small dark room.

After some time, Mr Hill apologised and took me out of jail. He asked why I was there and I explained the whole story.

"So when you went there, Robbie was already murdered, right," Mr Hill pondered. I nodded.

"And you saw someone there. Did Robbie have any domestic helpers?" he thoughtfully questioned.

"Yes, he has! Also, when I reached there, the hall was messed up, but everything was in place when you reached."

"The autopsy report came in today, and you got a clean chit. Robbie was stabbed using the kitchen knife. We received an anonymous call saying that Robbie was murdered. We couldn't track the number. But we tracked the phone's GPS last location and it was Robbie's house," Mr Hill unfolded.

I called the servants inside and felt I'd seen the butler somewhere. Shortsighted, almond-shaped eyes, big moustache, thick eyebrows...

"It's you," I shrieked.

The butler's eyebrows raised as he worriedly ran out of the room. I ran behind him and grabbed his shoulders. Then, pulling him back into the room, I yelled at him, "Why did you kill my friend!"

235

"I didn't kill anyone! I'll tell you the truth. I'd taken too many holidays, so sir refused to release my salary. I told him several times that my wife was sick, but he didn't believe me. So I thought of stealing. When I went into the room, sir had left for the hotel. However, when I was trying to open the safe, I heard someone coming towards the room, so I hit him," the butler deciphered. "I didn't know that it was you."

I went to Mr Hill's room and explained, "Let's send the servants' fingerprints to the forensic lab and inquire the hotel manager about his discussion with Robbie."

I drove to Parco Hotel, which was busy with the party. Finally, the manager arrived and explained the conversation in no time: "Mr Robbie came to ask about how the party was going on and then he left."

As I left the hotel, I received a call from James. One of the servant's fingerprints had matched, and a lady's bracelet was found at the crime scene. The bracelet was engraved with the initials of either someone's name or company.

I reached the bureau and handed Maria the bracelet. "Sir, this bracelet brand is 'Shoni'. This is a costly bracelet," Maria reported her research.

I ordered, "Maria, contact each of these store's managers and find out who had bought this bracelet. James, did you bring the hotel CCTV footage with you?"

"Sir, in this footage, at around 11 am, the manager left with Robbie."

"We'll have to go to the manager's house and ask him why he lied," I instructed.

James and I found the manager's house locked. The neighbour told us that he had left his house in a hurry.

We broke the door open and rummaged throughout the house. We found a Shoni receipt from his closet. James tracked the manager's phone number.

Soon, Maria phoned me, saying that she had found who had bought the bracelet and was going to fetch her.

They returned to the bureau with the manager and a lady I immediately recognised. It was the maid! James and Maria slapped them, forcing them to speak.

"He," she pointed towards the manager, "is my husband. Robbie would always humiliate my husband in front of everyone. He had got to know that we were selling the hotel's items and decided to fire my husband. That's when I decided to take revenge. I went as a maid in his house and made him trust me. That night he humiliated him again, so we both murdered him," she cried.

"We found your fingerprints on the knife. So now you will surely get life imprisonment for your crime," I yelled.

Suhani Thakur (13)

Tokyo Bay International School, Tokyo

The Project

As Nora and her best friend Sam were talking and thinking about ideas for their project that was due on Monday and trying to keep up with each other because of the Friday rush in the school hallway.

"Ugh... Why is everyone done with their projects except for us? We haven't started our documentary yet," said Nora to Sam as they reached their lockers.

Sam let out a deep sigh. "Let's start today; we only have the weekend to finish the whole documentary and I don't think that a parrot is hard to find and it's somewhere out there on Earth so do not make any other excuses in class," replied Sam, with a creaking, ear-hurting laugh while unlocking her locker.

Nora just rolled her eyes. "Alright, Sam, but please stop with the creaking, ear-hurting laugh, and what happens if our teacher gave us the parrot on purpose?" Nora asked.

"She wouldn't do it on purpose," replied Sam. "Hopefully."

Just then, Sam's older brother Matt walked into the hallway, flipping his brown hair and just then, Sam took out her flute and tried to hit Matt, but he dodged it.

"Wow, would you mind stopping the flute hitting? Please?" he asked in an angry voice.

"Fine, stop it with the hair flipping, it's weird, and it's embarrassing for me," replied Sam.

"Well, do you remember our talk about this? I'm not trying to embarrass you. So, could you both stop fighting, please?" Nova said, interrupting Matt.

Sam gave Nora her best angry look and Matt just ignored her.

"Well, does anybody want to go home?" asked Matt, pointing his thumb at the hallway traffic. "They should put signals in the hallways."

They reached Nora's house and, as Nora opened the door, they heard a loud motor noise. They went to check out the garage but when they opened the garage door, Matt slipped on a puddle of sticky, brownish-greenish liquid. The whole garage was covered in sticky, brownish-greenish liquid.

"Noah, what is all this? You know Mom will scold both of us if she sees this mess you have done!" said Nora in a high-pitch angry voice.

Noah, Nora's older brother, turned to them and then said, "If she figures it out and I won't let her. You alright, Matt?" Noah went to help Matt, and just at that moment, Nora had an idea.

Nora turned to Noah. "Um... hey, I got an idea. We won't tell Mom about this mess of yours if you take us to the nearby forest so Sam and I can finish making the documentary for our project. Deal?" asked Nora.

"That's a pretty good idea, but the only problem is that I don't think we're allowed to go inside the forest," said Sam looking around the room.

"We are allowed to go until a point," said Matt.

"Fine, we can go," replied Noah in a deep voice. "Since we're going to the forest, maybe we can camp out in the forest too. Also, I might need a little help cleaning up this mess."

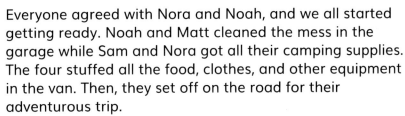

Everyone agreed with Nora and Noah, and we all started getting ready. Noah and Matt cleaned the mess in the garage while Sam and Nora got all their camping supplies. The four stuffed all the food, clothes, and other equipment in the van. Then, they set off on the road for their adventurous trip.

When they entered the forest, nothing was in sight, not even a cave or log cabin. We kept moving on an unpaved road; after a while, there was no road, just green grass. Sam was saying that maybe we should turn around and go back, but Matt, Noah and Nora insisted, so she had to agree to keep going. We kept going farther and farther from the city. Eventually, we decided it would be best if we took a reverse and went back home but Noah accidentally put the gear stick in drive instead of reverse, the van was at full speed and soon Noah had no control over the van.

Suddenly, a tree came in the way, so Noah quickly turned left. Everyone yelled. There was a broken and bent gate in front of us, and we were heading right towards it.

"Noah, careful, there's a gate," yelled Matt.

Before Noah could stop the van, we went on top of the bent gate and flew right through the branches of the trees. We landed with a big bang, and luckily they landed in the middle of a bunch of trees, making a large circle. Everyone was looking at each other in awe.

"Ah... we trespassed, we are trespassers," screamed Sam in a crying voice.

Sam unbuckled her seatbelt and opened the van's back door. She ran towards the broken gate. Luckily Nora stopped her before she could get any farther.

"Come on, Sam, you got to think about everyone else," said Nora. "Also, this gate looks even older closely."

Sam let out a deep sigh and followed Nora back to the van.

"Hey, Noah can U-turn and take us back home 'cause this place gives me the creeps," said Nora, tightening her seat belt.

"There's not enough space to turn. We have to keep moving. I've heard that a river leads back to our city to the left side of the forest. We need to find it and go back home."

Everyone agreed, so they went left as Noah had said. We kept going left, and soon it was sunset, so we decided we should stop and continue tomorrow. Just then, we hit something. Everyone thought it was a rock, so everyone climbed out of the van and saw a rusty train track.

We looked around and saw a building. We all got into the van excitedly because we found some kind of civilization, but we were wrong. It was a rusty old train station...

Mihika Bhalerao (11)

Tokyo Bay International School, Tokyo

The Killjoy

Once upon a time, there lived a boy named William. Will was the 2,834,455th person to be named Will to be born at that time. Will had a shadow like everything else in this world. His shadow's name was William 2,834,455b. A shadow is like a guardian who watches over you in your worst moments. He saves you from the most awkward situations, negotiates all your problems with other people, and helps you sail through this world unharmed and unscathed.

But Will's shadow was utterly different. He would offend everybody he met. People would run away crying, fight Will or be straight up, be obnoxious for no reason. Everybody would see Will's shadow and run away. They called him a Killjoy.

Will's typical day began with Killjoy kicking him awake (the boy always complained that he never woke up properly). Nobody liked Will because Killjoy would immediately start bullying other shadows, and it ended up reducing them to tears. This was the reason why he had no friends and no pets. He wanted to have a hound, play in the woods with his friends, and drift down lazy rivers dreaming of adventures, gold, and riches. But he couldn't.

First, he thought that something was wrong with his complexion. But when he looked in the mirror, he saw a tall, rugged youth with warm grey eyes caramel-coloured bangs and a playful smile. So, he pondered the idea that he wasn't smart enough. But he was top of the class; the whole world stayed cold and unfriendly. Eventually, Will gave up.

One day, Will was going to school, finding a coin, and pocketing it. His day was perfect! He became the most popular boy in school. He made lots of friends, enjoyed a wonderful afternoon, and went to feeling happy and content. And all because a little goblin came out of the coin and kicked Killjoy out.

The next day he was kicked awake by an even snappier Killjoy. His day was horrible; he preferred not to recall it. But, Will found out about lucky charms. And when Killjoy was on a break; he bought one. His day was perfect. Killjoy was out of his life, and there was no trace left of the timid small boy. Meanwhile, the Killjoy was slowly compressed and pushed out by the satanic creature that took its place. The seemingly harmless creature would erase its master's identity. They would let shadows slowly die unloved and unprotected.

But Will's Killjoy was unique, so he was able to leave a message for Will. And then Killjoy was off.

One day Will returned from baseball, high-fived his friends, and went into his bedroom to do his homework. He gave him a tape with a recording of the way they insulted a sixth grader making him run out crying.

As he listened to the tape, Killjoy's memory kicked in. It felt like he was disappearing, falling into a vast void, believing with all the memories spinning around him.

Moving increasingly faster until he was suspended in a hurricane above the whole world. And then he started falling back to his body.

He was sucked into a beautiful and terrible place where he saw every possibility. Where colours flooded his brain and eyes leaving him in harmony with the whole world. With a feeling of miraculous weightlessness that nobody could describe. Until he was sent back to Earth.

He collapsed in a heap, crying, broken from all that he saw. But he understood one thing: he had to bring his Killjoy. You can't throw away a part of yourself, no matter what. So, he lifted all the charms and lobbed them out of the window. And then he melted into a completely grey world. Will found himself in a vast white room with a statue of a robust knight. A recorded tape thundered out of his mouth.

"If you listen to this, you have committed a great sin. You have let your shadow be pushed out and humiliated by a being not worthy of your attention. You have exactly 24 hours to fix your mistake. Do not fail."

Will stood up, brushed off his jeans, took a deep breath, and exited into the world of shadows. The world of shadows is a miraculous place filled with only grey and black; it gives you the feeling of seeing a black and white film around you. Everything looks the same. So, a lot of times, you cannot tell any qualities.

Will witnessed this through the windows, in his bedroom, but everything was grey. After 5 minutes, there was nobody in sight. He thought that it might be easier to find his shadow. Surprisingly Will found the shadow reasonably quickly. Killjoy sat in Will's favourite place, sipping Will's favourite drink and looking forlornly at a wall. Will looked at Killjoy.

"Look, I'm sorry! I didn't mean to hurt you," said Will.
He waited for Killjoy to answer, but nothing happened.
"You know you aren't the easiest person to love; you can ruin the whole situation for no reason. It's annoying, and it hurts, so even you have to get why I did it."
Killjoy turned his head, and his eyes were devoid of empathy. From one look Will was thrown somewhere else, just like the massage. But unlike it, he didn't feel any harmony or safety. There were no things that kept him alive, loved, and worshipped with every second.
He was thrown further and further from what he loved and believed.
He could master only one word before he blacked out: "Sorry."
The next day he woke up being kicked awake by Killjoy.

Arina Soboleva (12)
Tokyo Bay International School, Tokyo

Pirates In Japan

In the night, a person called John was searching for treasure. He realised that the treasure was in Asia. This treasure was in Japan, so he started to search for treasure inside Japan.

He found the treasure, but it was in the middle of the street, so he began to find a person who could help him dig for the treasure.

After a few days, he found someone who could help him dig out the treasure from the street. It was near his house, which is called Wilmington in America. But he was a bad pirate. The pirates told John to give him half of the treasure if he got the treasure, and John agreed.

After a few weeks, they were ready to go. The pirate also took his crew. He took 12 crewmen, and they started their journey.

After they denatured, they calculated how many days they take to reach Japan. The answer was 60 days. Then John was surprised. He asked the crew if there was enough food and water for everyone. The crew said, "No!" and told him they would fish using land fishing rods. They said they would make fresh water from seawater.

John was a little nervous about this. So he started to read a book about survival techniques.

The sky was going to get dark, so they started to fish. They got so many fish in a few minutes that they began doing a barbecue. There was also some alcohol for them to drink, so they started to drink.

After some time, they got drunk and started to party. It was an excellent time to drink and enjoy.

It was past 11, so they went to their bedroom and slept.

The next day the crew felt confident, so they were energetic, so they started to make a gorgeous breakfast with yesterday's fish and little crabs roaming inside the ship. Then, they put the carbs and seaweed together to make soup and they made sushi with the fish. John felt that yummy and started to eat more.

Finally, he got full and more energetic, so he began researching his riding ship. He felt interested, so he started asking the pirate many questions.

After some time, the ship's sail suddenly got ripped, so everyone panicked, and they were getting the crew ready to climb up high to sew it up. It was a challenging moment because the ship was wiggling so much. It was hard to sew them up. It was successful. The crew could sew it up, but the hard time did not end.

The crew who went up could not come back. The rope which was tieing them up could not come out. So, they had the idea of shooting the rope and falling him down, but there was a problem. The idea was good, but the pirate's aim was bad. So, the pirate loaded the bullets into the gun and started to shoot the gun it didn't hit. Then John got the first try at shooting the gun.

First try, he shot the wooden bottle. He aimed it perfectly and shot it perfectly, so he found his new talent. On the second try, he shot the rope and it got hit perfectly through the rope. Then the pirate got suppressed and wanted to hire John as a crew member. But John didn't want to be a pirate, so he disagreed. He wanted to visit Japan to find treasure and help him dig it.

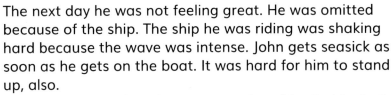

The next day he was not feeling great. He was omitted because of the ship. The ship he was riding was shaking hard because the wave was intense. John gets seasick as soon as he gets on the boat. It was hard for him to stand up, also.

Meanwhile, the other ship came to that ship. Suddenly the ship shot a cannon, attacking John's ship. But the ship was intact. But the ship wiggled so much, and so many crews fell. John also fell into the ocean.

But when John and the pirate realised they were in Japan! So he started to feature out where are they. They went to find a person who could speak English. He wrote: 'Can someone help us! Who can speak English?' on the paper and showed that to everyone in the city and they found a person who could speak English so, they were told to be with them. The person agreed, and she could translate them from English to Japanese.

So they went to a street where John found the treasure. There were so many pedestrians and cars, so digging a hole and taking the treasure was complicated. But the lady who could speak English knew there was a small tunnel where they could go under that street.

They go to the tunnel where you can go into the place you can go under the road and they quickly find the treasure there. They were happy to see that treasure there and decided to divide it into three.

They then happily went back to their house.

Bigen Thapa

Tokyo Bay International School, Tokyo

Why Is Technology Dangerous And Useful For Humans?

Technology results from accumulated knowledge and application of skills, methods and processes in industrial production and scientific research.

Technology is embedded in the operation of all machines and electronic devices, with or without detailed knowledge of their function, for the intended purpose of an organisation. The technologies of society consist of what are known as systems. Systems operate by obtaining an input, altering this input through what is known as a process, and then producing an outcome that achieves the system's intended purpose.

Technology is used to exchange information, clean our clothes, prepare our meals and get from one place to another. But even everyday items like door locks, floor panels, and furniture are technologies that we now take for granted, which seem less impressive to us than self-driving cars or 3D printing.

The danger of technology: social media and mobile devices may lead to psychological and physical issues, such as eyestrain and difficulty focusing on essential tasks. They may also contribute to more severe health conditions, such as depression. The overuse of technology may have a more significant impact on developing children and teenagers.

Kadhir Karthikeyan (13)
Tokyo Bay International School, Tokyo

The Five Elements

Once there lived the five elements. Their names were Fire, Water, Air, Sky and Land. Now, Fire and Water didn't get along. As you know, Water can put out Fire, and Fire can burn Water.

Fire and Water kept quarrelling and disputing. Their fighting never seemed to stop. Fire kept burning Water's lakes, rivers, ponds, and oceans, and Water kept putting out small campfires or the big fires in the Everglades that Fire created. This caused significant problems all around the Earth, causing droughts in some places or big fires in others.

Air, Sky, and Land got along just fine, but they hated fighting Fire and Water. And once they realised that Fire and Water were causing so many problems on the Earth, they decided themselves that they couldn't start fighting or that the Earth would be in chaos. So, Air and Sky decided to go along with the plan.

The next day, when Fire and Water started fighting, Air, Sky and Land executed their plan, shopping! The three shouted loud enough so Fire and Water could hear, "We're going shopping. Bye!"

The next thing they knew, Fire and Water were going with them. You wouldn't believe it, but there was a whole world above the clouds just for the elements. And not just the five elements, but there were more elements.

When the five elements reached the Shopping centre, they all went their ways. For example, Land went to the brown and Earthy dresses, Air went to the white and light ones and Sky went to the blue and white ones. They all had their ways!

Suddenly, Water and Fire met in the same place. A place with a beautiful purple dress with both of the girl's styles was amazingly flowy, which suited Water's style, and little red and blue gemstones along the waist suited Fire's style. It was both their second favourite colour: Purple! After all, red and blue make purple.

When the girls met in that place with the stunning purple dress, they started tugging it. But after a few minutes of tugging, they both started laughing. They both apologised to each other and started talking. It was like the magic of shopping brought them together.

Then miraculously, they went to the shopkeeper together and asked for another one of those purple dresses. Fortunately, it was the last one they had in the stockroom. So, the two girls both got their purple dresses.

Once all five elements gathered outside the store, Sky and Air were surprised to see the plan worked. They were most surprised by was that Fire and Water were chatting away like they had been friends for two thousand and twenty-three years of their lives. (Spirits have immortality - you are pretty young, when you are two thousand and twenty-three years old in immortal life, maybe 14 in human years?). But they were happy that their plan worked as the Earth was not in chaos anymore.

Fire and Water realised how much they had in common. They were surprised themselves how much they had in common. They promised on Spirtualla (the name for the spirit world and which is a significant promise), that they would never fight again in their immortal lives, and they had a great life, both the five elements and the mortals.

Prajitha Sri Madhumitha Prathieesh

Tokyo Bay International School, Tokyo

What Do Values Mean To You?

The first question I asked myself was, "What is a value?" According to the dictionary, it means the monetary worth of something and the market price of the good. But by the age of 8, I learned people have different values.

Where do people learn their moral values? The value they learn throughout life is learned at an early age. Also, children get influenced by their teachers and parents. Furthermore, families and educators play the most crucial role in building values in children and students as they become their role models.

Childhood and the teenage period are the most critical phases as they decide the person's moral value for the rest of their lives. Also, literacy is key to having good moral values. Education without values tends to make a person miserable. Electronic gadgets and mobile apps have changed the methods of learning.

Children are used to the online education atmosphere. As the pandemic's effect diminishes, they have started attending offline classes. But we see nowadays that they have less regard for their mentors and are glued to their pads and laptops. (Source: Vedanta)

Value is essential to life as it can change a person's life. A person with good values is universally loved, contrasting with people harbouring wrong values. Values are based on various ideas and situations. While the fundamental values remain the same across cultures and have been intact for centuries, some values change with differing factors.

Family plays the most crucial role in giving us a sense of value. Decisions in life are largely based on the values we have. A person is always known by the values he possesses. The values of a person always reflect on his attitude and personality. Moral values are fading these days. The young generation is busy taking care of their career and enjoying life. Older adults are often neglected. Sometimes there are cases of young people mistreating their ageing parents or even evicting them.

Due to the highly competitive life, even small children are neglected. The culture threshold is lowering daily due to the effect of western influence and television programs which often mislead the younger generation.

While everyone knows that values are essential, the world is changing rapidly. So, parents are busy making money for the family and living a good lifestyle that they overlook the importance of value.

At the age when children must be taught good values, they are taught to fight and survive in this competitive world. As a result, their academics and performance in other activities are given importance over their values.

Society depends on whether the person contributing to the society have similar value. In making a better society, priority must be given to child's life because they are the future.

Society will be in the best shape when people show ethical values and act for good.

Rahad Al Safa (14)

Tokyo Bay International School, Tokyo

Summer

It's August
It's summer
Time to go out
The public transport
Are full of people travelling
Also, the best time to swim
It's the best time to go out
It's the best time to travel
And the best time to swim
Summer, it's the best.

Kai Nakamura (10)
Tokyo Bay International School, Tokyo

The Corridor

The door creaked open, the smell of metal fading away. She glanced back at the place she called home for the last night, the plain bunk beds only casting a shadow between the crack of sunlight.

The girl held the torch and placed her foot forward, swallowing. Where was she?

Noise was escaping from the next corridor, but who were they talking to?

The sound echoed through the walls, causing her ears to bleed.

Her torch now flickered, her heart pounding through her chest as she broke into a run. Corridor after corridor but no exit. No escape.

The girl raised her head, the tall dark walls surely guaranteeing a death - but from what?

A haunting chill rose upon her neck as she turned around. A black figure stood. The only exit was tracing back her steps. Yelling to no one in particular she ran; thankful for the boost of adrenaline. She was trying to think of her family at home - wherever home was.

Lost, she fell to the ground and rocked her legs like a cradle. No memory was coming back. Who even was she?

Molly Nash (13)

Trafalgar School, Hilsea

The Man

Alone, the man sat, the cold steel of the rifle pressed on the back of his neck, a stream of tears slowly moving down his face. He had already written the note and had planned the whole thing but he couldn't bring himself to do it, to end it as soon as it started, to lose what he loved and for others to lose him forever. He closed his eyes and pulled the trigger but the rifle jammed, he wanted to go but fate made him stay, maybe he should live on for the rest of the week and see what happened?

The next day he woke up and did his morning routine (shower, workout and watch TV until he had to leave). On his way to his soul-sucking 9 to 5 he stopped to buy a coffee at the coffee shop then continued his walk to work. As he sat in his bland cubicle, working on his computer, his phone rang (nothing usual). He picked up expecting Martha from accounting or his boss Derek complaining about his work, but today was different, a young voice said over the phone, "Do you want to escape your boring job?" The man hung up. *Another spam caller*, he thought.

At 5 o'clock, he left his job and went to the car dealership across town, he entered the dealership and asked about the shiny red car in the window. He was told it was the newest model, he said, "I'll take it," handed the salesman a wad of cash and drove the car off the lot. He drove home, smiling along the way and listening to the radio. He got home and went to sleep, pleased with his new car.

The next day he drove the car to work, everyone looked at him in awe at the shiny new car. As he entered the office with a big grin, his boss walked up to him, happiness in his eyes, the man was demoted.

As he finished moving his stuff into the different office he noticed the time was 5:30 so he left, exited to drive in his new car, when he saw the car was broken into and the wheels and radio were stolen and the car's paint was scratched off. He walked home saddened, when he saw on his door an eviction notice. He entered his house, tears in his eyes grabbed the pre-written note and the rifle sat down on his bed and pulled the trigger. His sad week had ended just as it started.

Alfie Appleton (13)

Trafalgar School, Hilsea

Our Holiday

As the boat arrived at the ferry port we drove onto the boat and got out of the car. On the boat we went to the sweet shop and got what we wanted, after we went to get drinks and sat on the chairs in the boat by the window, it began to get dark so we went out on the deck before we came back inside and went to sleep.

The next morning the ferry arrived at the French ferry port, I stepped off the ferry, and the warm breeze hit me, I could smell the saltwater right next to me. I could see the ice cream shop with all the amazing flavours, the water slides had children sliding down them, screaming. The sun was beaming down on me, I could see people riding around on bikes. The huge, clear lake shimmered as people went around on paddle boards and jumped into the warm water. As it got to three o'clock it got to thirty-five degrees. The beaches had soft sand under my feet, the small waves washed up against the sand. I watched people swimming in the calm sea.

Isabella Boyd (12)
Trafalgar School, Hilsea

Anticipation Of Winter

Cold mornings.
Cosy nights.
Bedroom window frosty, blocking the daylight.

So cold outside of these covers,
I don't want to move.
Until I remember it's my favourite time of year.

Halloween, Bonfire Night and Christmas too.
Watching movies with my family.

Hot chocolate, popcorn with blankets all around.
While the slippery ice-coated streets don't make a sound.

The snow starts to slowly fall,
Like miniature balls of felt.
Outside we run and pray,
It doesn't quickly melt.

Outside our warm breath meets the cold.
Smoke blowing out, it never gets old.

Anticipation of winter,
It's my favourite time of year.
I get excited every time it's near.

Bentley Blu McGee-Osundo (12)
Trafalgar School, Hilsea

The Circus

I went to the circus on Thursday at 5pm. I went with my mum, sister and auntie. My mum bought me a big candyfloss, it was very sticky. At the circus my mum told me to look up and I saw a man above me. He was walking on a tightrope very fast. After the tightrope act there was a funny clown who threw popcorn on people and got them with a water hose. My favourite act was the one with the motorbikes in a cage. Three motorbikes went in, they went fast, going round and round and round. While I was watching them, I felt something touch my leg. I looked down and I saw it was the clown.
I had a fantastic time that day.

Finlay Roxburgh (11)
Trafalgar School, Hilsea

Star Tea Party

Moonlight glistens, reigning forever
Star attendees gather together
A deity chanting a melody.
Chirping devotion whistles the atmosphere.
Gossiping all night, midnight fall,
Teatime for them; a party has begun,
Let us commemorate with copious fun.
Whilst chitter chatter goes pitter patter.
Peculiarity flickers within the distance.
A solitary luminosity weeps alone.
A radiance of a different glow; outcast from them all.
One that will make them all recall, the spectacular ball.

Come now, little one. For your time shall come.
When you'll be the centre of everyone.
With your funny laugh and lovely smile,
Up and foremost they'll understand you're worthwhile.
The bustling and booming festivity glistens bright.
Little one, don't feel fright. It's alright.
Although you may be misconceived toneless,
As you deep down grow,
You're reserved for honest faithfulness.
Only one that you'll know.

The witching hour is struck by midnight,
Discourse drizzles and evaporates.
For now our hostess has spoken.

Her words mirror, selecting one.
Perhaps a guessing game for everyone?
For what she seeks is not yet shown.
Eyeing all of them, to find a whim.
Now, the real story will begin.
Demanding for someone to designate.
Someone whose heart is true.
That's strange, I thought this was about you...?
Guessing who; chitter chatter.
A delightful rose hidden within thorns.
One that cannot easily burst,
Woefully one that locks away the true beauty.
A beauty protecting itself in fear.
Tittle-tattle in shock.
For she is not requiring any looks of sorts,
As looks do not define her wishes.
All she seeks is a unique glow.
A new variant of flower.
There, perhaps over there,
There? Where?
Silence erupts one by one.
See, I told you!
The real story had begun.
For one day, someone would come to know,
That gentle beauty down below.
For here she will announce,

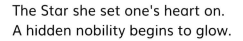

The Star she set one's heart on.
A hidden nobility begins to glow.

Ah, so now you know!
For no matter your looks, feeling or might.
Every star will sparkle one night.
If a little belief is put in,
What can we make begin?
Patience will be a virtue.
As your new chapter begins, remember it, won't you?

Elise Griffin
Voyage Learning Campus Milton, Worle

Forgive Me

We were inseparable.
They've been with me since I last remember.
I've been with them since the beginning of their journey.

They carried me through all the tough times,
The sad, the happy ones too.
The ones I remember most,
As well as the ones that will haunt me forever too.

I remember the day we met, it's something I'll never forget.

Not a hello or a welcome -
Just a benevolent warm embrace.
They taught me manners, patience,
And most of all grace.
They strike me as quite unique
Yet impossibly small.
They were proud of me,
And made me stand tall.

It was you who made me who I am now - I owe you it all.

But forgive me,
I know I've made a mistake.
I threw you away -
Like a heartless snake.

I left you to rot and die,
As we grew apart.

I just want to say thank you -

And that you'll always have a place in my heart.

Heba Omar (13)
Whalley Range High School, Whalley Range

Princesses

Macy turns to me, "Olivia what do you want to watch
tonight?"
We have all the Disney princesses, even my favourite,
Snow White!
But I have no interest in their frilly dresses and golden
locks,
When these girls enter the real world, they'll be in for a
shock!
They portray Disney girls as helpless, pretty dolls,
When they meet them in person, they will see the truth
unfold,

Let's start with Snow,
And her pretty red bow,
Runs away from the evil queen,
And goes to seven men to cook and clean,
Expecting her prince, that's so out of reach,
This is the opposite of what we want to preach!

Next on to Cinderella,
Again, another one after a handsome fella,
Has two evil stepsisters who go to the ball,
They make her a slave as she sobs feeling so small,
But her fairy godmother uses her tricks,
So, Cindy can go to the ball and find her prince,
She loses her shoe at the stroke of midnight,
And gives the prince such a fright!

So he goes around half the world,
To return the shoe to the pretty girl,
Finally, they reunite,
She tries on the shoe, and it fits exactly right.
Good old Cindy now has a happy life,
With the prince and becomes a lovely wife,
It's pathetic how they need a handsome gent,
These movies are exactly what we need to prevent!

Now Sleeping Beauty,
Another one after her prince,
He needs to wake her up with a dramatic kiss,
Maleficent is the evil one,
Sets a sleeping curse on Aurora, for fun
It is ridiculous that princesses are portrayed this way,
They will find out that it is not true one day,
Us girls are independent when will they see?
This is not how girls should be looked at in society!
Anyway of course he gives her a true love kiss,
They live happily together Aurora and the prince,

Next up is our French girl Belle,
Another story I am reluctant to tell,
A handsome prince cruelly turned into a beast,
Who takes out his fury on the lovely little girl he meets,
The rose petal in the forbidden room must fall,
For the horrific-looking beast to go back to normal,
The Beast holds Belle hostage we don't know how long for,

Belle starts realising she's falling for the Beast more
and more,
A true love kiss comes up again,
Am I the only one that is being driven insane?
Of course, the Beast is now a prince,
Him and Belle haven't been seen since,
I can't tell any of the movies apart,
They all begin with a broken heart,
Who finds their man and lives happily,
Are you seriously trying to fool me?

Rapunzel the girl we know as the one with long hair,
Rapunzel, guess what I just do not care,
You got taken away by Mother Gothel,
Who uses your hair to keep her young and small,
The prince is your saviour,
And saves you from the danger,
These movies, they just are not right,
All they care about is if she is a pretty sight,

"So, what about Moana?" I cleverly suggest,
"She is not putting on a show or there to impress,"
Or Merida, she is not the stereotypical princess you see,
She follows her dreams and is who she wants to be,
But all your pretty princesses to me look the same,
And Disney with no regrets it is you I blame,
For all the young girls who hate the look of their face,
And when they look at their bodies they see a disgrace,

You should not be insecure at such an early age,
Because of the way Disney girls are portrayed,

You do not need a man, you're great on your own,
You do not need a prince next to you on your throne,
Polish your tiara and wear it with pride,
Push Disney's expectation of you aside,

Be proud of the strong women you will be,
And tell yourself, I do not need a true love's kiss
to define me!

Olivia Cooper (13)
Yavneh College, Borehamwood

Refugee Poem

Say this city has 5 million souls
Some of us are living in castles while others are living
in holes
Once before we had a country which is now destroyed
So, we must wait here to fill the void

We were just sitting in school, it was just a usual day
But then all of a sudden the sky turned grey
We were told to hide under the table and chairs
This is so scary, I can't even bear.

We were told to run home as fast as we could
And when I got there, I was greeted with a pile of brick
and wood
Luckily Mum had managed to pack
My most special things, which I could carry on my back

On my way to the border, to cross over
I wish I was getting a ferry to Dover
Instead, I hope they allow me into Poland today
All I can do is sit here and pray

As we travel our way through
I can't quite believe what's happening, we are the lucky few
We pass countryside, cattle and another landmark
It stops for other strangers to embark

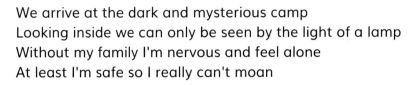

We arrive at the dark and mysterious camp
Looking inside we can only be seen by the light of a lamp
Without my family I'm nervous and feel alone
At least I'm safe so I really can't moan

Suddenly, well-dressed people walk in
Waiting to be picked is like a lottery win
The families come to choose a refugee to stay
Will this be my lucky day?

I settle well with my host family in my temporary home
A call from my dad so I pick up my phone
It's great to hear a familiar voice to remind me of the past
I hope this call won't be the last

Despite feeling safe, I still miss my previous abode
My new life is so different, it's a very heavy load
I have such conflicting emotions, as I'm safe and well
All I want to hear is my old school bell.

Sasha Osterley (12)
Yavneh College, Borehamwood

YoungWriters®
Est. 1991

YOUNG WRITERS
INFORMATION

We hope you have enjoyed reading this book – and that you will continue to in the coming years.

If you're a young writer who enjoys reading and creative writing, or the parent of an enthusiastic poet or story writer, do visit our website **www.youngwriters.co.uk**. Here you will find free competitions, workshops and games, as well as recommended reads, a poetry glossary and our blog. There's lots to keep budding writers motivated to write!

If you would like to order further copies of this book, or any of our other titles, then please give us a call or order via your online account.

Young Writers
Remus House
Coltsfoot Drive
Peterborough
PE2 9BF
(01733) 890066
info@youngwriters.co.uk

Join in the conversation!
Tips, news, giveaways and much more!

 YoungWritersUK YoungWritersCW youngwriterscw